®

teach
yourself

getting started in
the Second Life world

GW00771701

getting started in
the Second Life world

irie tsure

Launched in 1938, the **teach yourself** series
grew rapidly in response to the world's
wartime needs. Loved and trusted by over 50
million readers, the series has continued to
respond to society's changing interests and
passions and now, 70 years on, includes over
500 titles, from Arabic and Beekeeping to
Yoga and Zulu. What would you like to learn?

Be where you want to be with **teach yourself**

For UK order enquiries: please contact Bookpoint Ltd, 130 Milton Park, Abingdon, Oxon OX14 4SB. Telephone: +44 (0)1235 827720. Fax: +44 (0)1235 400454. Lines are open 09.00–17.00, Monday to Saturday, with a 24-hour message answering service. Details about our titles and how to order are available at www.teachyourself.co.uk.

For USA order enquiries: please contact McGraw-Hill Customer Services, PO Box 545, Blacklick, OH 43004-0545, USA. Telephone: 1-800-722-4726. Fax: 1-614-755-5645.

For Canada order enquiries: please contact McGraw-Hill Ryerson Ltd, 300 Water St, Whitby, Ontario L1N 9B6, Canada. Telephone: 905 430 5000. Fax: 905 430 5020.

Long renowned as the authoritative source for self-guided learning – with more than 50 million copies sold worldwide – the **teach yourself** series includes over 500 titles in the fields of languages, crafts, hobbies, business, computing and education.

British Library Cataloguing in Publication Data: a catalogue record for this title is available from The British Library.

Library of Congress Catalog Card Number: on file.

First published in UK 2008 by Hodder Education, part of Hachette Livre UK, 338 Euston Road, London NW1 3BH.

First published in USA 2008 by The McGraw-Hill Companies Inc.

The **teach yourself** name is a registered trademark of Hodder Headline.

Computer hardware and software brand names mentioned in this book are protected by their respective trademarks and are acknowledged.

Notice and Disclaimer. Linden Lab and Second Life are trademarks of Linden Research, Inc. Teach Yourself Getting Started in the Second Life World is not affiliated with or sponsored by Linden Research.

The publisher has used its best endeavours to ensure that the URLs for external websites referred to in this book are correct and active at the time of going to press. However, the publisher has no responsibility for the websites and can give no guarantee that a site will remain live or that the content is or will remain appropriate.

Typeset by Mac Bride, Southampton

Printed in Great Britain for Hodder Education, an Hachette Livre UK Company, 338 Euston Road, London NW1 3BH, by CPI Cox & Wyman, Reading, Berkshire RG18EX.

Hachette Livre UK's policy is to use papers that are natural, renewable and recyclable products and made from wood grown in sustainable forests. The logging and manufacturing processes are expected to conform to the environmental regulations of the country of origin.

Impression number   10 9 8 7 6 5 4 3 2 1

Year   2011 2010 2009 2008

contents

For

Violet, Jem, Jasper, Jenson and Jada

(You are my First Life)

A friend told me about Second Life®. 'It's the next big thing!' she said. So on 22 September 2006 I downloaded the Second Life software (the *viewer*), created an appalling looking 'mini-me' (know as an *avatar*) then pursued the common strategy of wandering around aimlessly. I spoke with a few people. They seemed less interested in me than I was in them. I visited the popular places but the visions that greeted me didn't inspire me to hang around. After a few hours I had become bored. I informed my friend that Second Life was not for me. She peered over my shoulder to inspect my pitiful excuse for an avatar. It had been my intention to create a personal representative in cyberspace; my own proxy if you will. 'This is supposed to be your second life,' she said. 'That avatar looks just like you!'

Irie tip

I dearly wish I could show you images of my early days here but I was utterly and disappointingly unfamiliar with Second Life's simple but brilliant camera feature. Assuming that you have the necessary space on your system hard drive (saving your captured images to your hard drive carries no cost), I advise that from the first moment you step into the Second Life world that you regularly capture images of your own Second Life experience by clicking the Snapshot button on the viewer's bottom menu bar (see Chapter 5 for more).

'A second life?!' I digested the concept for a few moments. My imagination fired. I radically altered my appearance. I gave my avatar a new style and bestowed upon her a few character traits that in real life I just don't possess. I spoke with a different syntax. I turned my proxy into a character.

And then I began to role-play and continue to do so to this day, so when you ask me where I am from, I will respond with 'I live here!' for Irie Tsure was born in Second Life and does not exist anywhere else.

For me interacting 'in character' is stimulating. I am someone I am not. I can say anything that I wish, respond in any way and invent any aspect of my history. I am sometimes acting and sometimes I am not. It's rather like improvising a character from within a perpetual soap opera and like any good scriptwriter, I rarely let my own reality get in the way of a good story.

But I can and do share important and personal aspects of my real life. My best friend died last year and I moved home six months later. I shared these significant life moments in-world as I needed the support of good friends to carry me through.

I also vocalize my real world views (often to the chagrin of our members), my dreams, celebrate my good days and rant during my not so good days; these and many other personal areas of my life I share with other Second Life residents perhaps with an intimacy and with a comfort greater than when face to face with scary reality. This is how I have chosen to operate in cyberspace. You will develop your own survival strategy.

Like all good *newbies* (a resident new to Second Life), I typed 'free' into the search box and started gathering all the *freebies* (free stuff) I could find. Within a couple of weeks I registered for a premium account then added (if I remember correctly) £10 to my account (my only ever real world financial investment) with which I bought some Linden dollars. I then bought my first virtual land. I had collected some free prefab homes on my journeys, found one I liked, erected my first home on my first land and began furnishing.

It is apparent that I am more interesting in my second life for on my travels I started to make a few friends. I discovered how to modify my home and as I was going to need an income, also installed a small store on the ground floor exhibiting some 'art' that I had learned to create. I sold this art mainly to friends but also to occasional passers by. A short time later I bought the adjacent parcel with my profits and extended the store. Within a month I was again in a position to buy more land. By this time my building and texturing, though basic, had become more practised and on my latest land acquisition I built three homes; one for me and two to endeavour to rent to other residents.

I love music and discovered I could easily set an Internet reggae radio station to broadcast music across my land parcel. I also love to dance so in front of the rental homes I installed a little freebie dance floor that I had previously collected. I particularly love to chill so I created some simple beanbags and placed some beside this dance floor. I had named the art gallery *Irie Dreamz* so in turn named this little communal space *Irie Vibes*. Friends came to visit me at Irie Vibes from time to time, other people passed by and then more people came. So I created an Irie Vibes *group* and our very own community was officially born.

During my first year in Second Life I enjoyed learning to build and create objects. I have a passion for learning and the Second Life platform provides me with an opportunity to develop a vast array of skills in which I have had little or no previous experience. I acquired these skills as I needed them and therefore the overall learning process has been quite random. At the end of my first year in-world there remained a large gap in my knowledge. It was only once I had committed to writing a chapter on scripting for this book that I dared to tackle the daunting task of understanding the Linden's mysterious scripting language (LSL).

The skills of building, texturing and scripting appear mystical even to many long-term residents of Second Life. *Time Magazine* wrote that 'As on many sites, there's a learning curve for novices, but Second Life's is simply too steep'. The reality is that in Second Life, and to the credit and kudos of the team at Linden Lab, all the skills (including scripting) are extraordinarily simple to grasp, learn and develop once they are explained clearly and in a logical order. This book intends to demystify the skills you will require to prosper within your Second Life, in an order most conducive to easy understanding and rapid development.

Your only requirements are the knowledge of how to use your mouse and keyboard, some time and an appetite to learn.

Bon voyage.

Irie Tsure Xxx

acknowledgements

Little of my own learning would have been possible without considerable input from the many contributors to the Second Life Knowledgebase, The Second Life Wiki, the LSL Portal and the LSL Wiki.

I am humbled by the love and generous support of my friends **Redgold Greene, Mariboo Boa, Annc Idziak, Eve Parnall, Irie Iwish** and **Alan Miller**.

I appreciate the hard work and time spent by my proofreaders cum technical advisers **Sandro Sonnenblume** and **Zib Scaggs** as well as **ZamBowi Yifu** for patiently posing for the cover image.

I thank **Mike Calvert** and **Jade Hannya** for being my original Second Life friends and for encouraging, supporting and looking after me since my arrival.

I thank the Staff, DJs and Members of the global 'Irie Vibes' community who collectively and daily inspire and motivate me to learn more, create more and provide more with their love, wit, wisdom, support, challenges and strengths.

I thank Linden Labs, their staff and the residents of Second Life for giving me a platform and a voice.

Finally but above all I thank my family who, though often bewildered, support me with almost no question. I love you, learn most from you and don't deserve you.

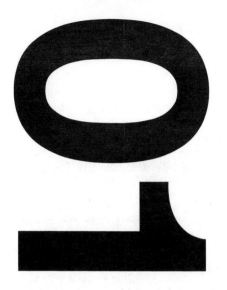

01

an overview of second life

In this chapter you will learn:

- about Second Life
- why other people are here

What is Second Life?

A virtual world is a computer simulated environment in which the user is represented by a computer-generated character known as an *avatar*. Until recently, virtual worlds were most commonly confined locally to the user's own computer system. *The Sims*® would be the perfect example of a popular but local virtual world.

Second Life operates as a virtual world but by networking through the Internet is simultaneously and permanently populated by tens of thousands of users from around the real world. These users of Second Life are referred to as the *residents*.

Downloadable software (the *viewer*) enables residents of Second Life to view, interact and explore the virtual world. Residents use the viewer to communicate, to participate in individual and group activities and to create objects. Residents can trade these objects or other services using the local Second Life currency; the *Linden dollar*.

Many aspects of the Second Life virtual world appear similar to the real world. Real world rules that apply in-world include persistent time (i.e. it continues when you are not there), gravity, sun cycles, physics (movement and collisions), light and reflection, topography, weather, economics, real-time actions and communication. Communications were originally managed exclusively in the form of typed text but now real-time voice communication is an available feature within Second Life.

The Second Life virtual world was developed by San Francisco based Linden Research Inc. (commonly referred to as Linden Lab or LL) and opened to the public in 2003.

The Second Life world is simulated on an array of computer servers referred to as *the grid*. This is divided into thousands of uniquely named *regions* (each commonly referred to as a *sim*). Each region measures 256 × 256 metres in-world and runs on its own CPU (Central Processing Unit). Regions can be, and usually are, divided into smaller individually named *parcels* of land.

Sometimes and often contentiously referred to as a game, Second Life is indeed an environment where people can undertake activities for the purpose of personal enjoyment but it does not possess many of the characteristics commonly attributed to games or gaming. Second Life does not award points, keep scores, judge winners and losers, provide levels to complete or profess an end-strategy.

What do residents do in Second Life?

'Your World, Your Imagination'

The strap-line adopted by the Second Life brand perfectly reflects the essence of Second Life. It offers residents possibilities and opportunities in which we are only limited by the reaches of our thinking. We each choose, with a freedom not possible in the real world, who we are, how we will live here and what we will do with our time.

The social dimension of Second Life is the feature seized upon by most residents. Entering a new social world is easily achieved by visiting a specific or themed venue, by entering a role-playing environment or joining a group. It is almost impossible for residents not to quickly form a group of like-minded friends then quickly become entwined within the rich social tapestry that Second Life provides.

Many residents purchase virtual land allowing them to open virtual businesses or create their own virtual spaces and homes. The Second Life platform has also been identified as a cutting-edge classroom for colleges and universities such as the Open University (UK), Harvard University, University College Dublin and the AFEKA Tel Aviv Academic College of Engineering.

Some residents visit the Second Life grid only once or twice, find no attraction and quickly leave. Others, like myself (after a week or two of orientation), find themselves drawn into the environment and spend many hours every day in-world. People become long-term residents of Second Life for a multitude of reasons.

It's the world's greatest chat-room!

Many Internet users familiar with chat-rooms will find the Second Life experience infinitely more stimulating. Immersed in a 3D space, residents of Second Life can express themselves through their avatar appearance, shape and attire. Avatars can express themselves further and even interact with other residents using animations such as distinct walks, dances and hugs. If you like chat-rooms then you are going to love Second Life!

It's creative heaven

Creativity in Second Life is initially expressed by all residents in terms of avatars' appearances and shapes. Residents also create avatar accessories including but not limited to clothes, hair, footwear, tattoos, jewellery and skin. Residents also design and build furniture and the buildings that contain them. Residents landscape their parks and gardens. In fact it is the residents that create all of the content for Second Life.

The building tools built into the Second Life viewer allow for the creation and manipulation of basic 3D shapes such as boxes, pyramids and spheres. These *prims* (primitive shapes) can be stretched, refined, cut, re-textured, linked into more complex forms and have physical qualities such as light and flexibility attributed to them. Building skills are easy to learn and enable residents to create an unending supply of objects.

Scripts can be added to objects. A script is a small chunk of computer code that enables an object to perform a task or function. We will introduce scripts and scripting more clearly in the following chapters so please do not worry at this stage if you have no idea of what a script is or what it does. All will be revealed in due course.

Creativity can also be expressed through photography, video or *Machinima*. Machinima is movie-making within a real-time, 3D virtual environment and Second Life provides a perfect base as it permits a low-cost and time-efficient way to produce movies whilst maintaining a high degree of creative control. Versatile cameras and recorders are built into the Second Life viewer for these purposes.

Downloading free and widely available software also enables residents to create content that can be imported into Second Life. Subject to certain simple parameters, your own animations, textures (images), sounds and even objects can all be easily imported into Second Life.

Established and emerging performers, DJs and musicians from all genres and all corners of the real world are finding performance and creative opportunities within Second Life. Jay-Z, Suzanne Vega, Chamillionaire, Avril Lavigne and 100s of up and coming artists have all performed live in Second Life.

It's great fun

If you are not feeling creative, Second Life provides an almost limitless range of other things to do. Visit a nightclub or funfair, go shopping, meditate in a crystal room, walk along deserted beaches or explore enchanted forests. Play chess up close and personal with your Internet opponent or get involved in a grid-wide, themed or role-playing game. There are thousands of easy-to-find events listed every day and there is an easy-to-use search facility incorporated into the Second Life viewer.

It's a perfect escape

'I'm not disabled in Second Life!' Kat

'Not disabled' could of course be substituted in Kat's enlightening statement with 'not chronically ill', 'less lonely', 'not deaf', 'not suffering from depression', 'not trapped as a carer', 'not housebound', 'not agoraphobic', 'not stigmatized', 'not judged by my appearance' or not marginalized by any of many other common and less common human sufferings.

The ability to access an unfettered second existence and fully participate within such a vast creative and social structure from the relative comfort of one's own PC has proved an escape for many individuals challenged in real life by social exclusion, disability or illness. A little user experience will demonstrate to you just how quickly and deeply connected users become to their own avatar and just how immersive the environment becomes. Therefore disabled and socially excluded individuals can find their place in Second Life alongside the general population and leave behind many earthly burdens. Kat currently dances for hours every day in the dance halls of Second Life 'just for the joy of moving'.

I've learned that the significant challenges some residents must bear preclude them from working in the real world. Forget the finances; it is 'purpose', the 'belonging to a team' and the 'contributing to one's society' that are the personal rewards many of these socially excluded individuals miss most.

Getting a job or building a business in Second Life not only offers an opportunity to earn some money and to make a meaningful contribution to this society but also provides a personal motivating force in as much as, very quickly, the choice of whether to log on or not becomes replaced by pressing Second Life duties, commitments and responsibilities.

I'm not a psychologist and I have no idea whether the experts feel it is largely a positive or negative pastime for an individual to escape to a virtual world. What I do know is that when I was informed that a resident, seemingly well in Second Life, had died of cancer, it quickly dawned on me that she had opted to spend the majority of her final months as a healthy, fit, able, active and socially functioning individual, in a beautiful, tropical, welcoming and pain-free world. Within Second Life, Khady never spoke of her cancer and therefore was neither defined as a victim nor marginalized by her suffering. Within Second Life, Khady was free to choose to spend her time as an impossibly carefree, vibrant and important part of our community; and we miss her.

Education

Offering a platform for cooperative work, simulation and training, the Second Life grid provides a uniquely flexible environment for educators and students as well as allowing educational institutions to provide learning opportunities that offer a sense of presence and engagement to distant students who may otherwise feel isolated. From within a virtual classroom, students can collaborate on online projects and teachers can present lectures from anywhere in the world.

To encourage educational usage of the grid, Second Life have established a non-profit and educators' programme which allows qualifying organizations to benefit from discounted land rates and access to group mailing lists.

Using the Second Life platform as a supplement to traditional teaching methods provides educators with opportunities for enriching an existing curriculum in areas such as the following.

Business Studies

The macro nature of the Second Life economy, combined with the viewer's functionality, provide an ideal platform for low-cost enterprise education. Students can work together to research the market, design, develop, introduce, then promote a product, service or event. Within these projects, students can be assigned specific roles not limited to builders, scripters, designers, marketing executives, performers, hosts and management.

Modern Languages

The Second Life virtual world uses both a text-based chat system and a voice chat function and therefore language students can practise both the writing and speaking skills of modern languages. The text-based chat system supports many language character sets and the grid is populated by numerous nationalities and cultures, many represented within their own regions. Teachers and students can visit representations of nations and cultures as well as national museums and cultural exhibitions from around the globe; virtual school trips without the prohibitions of cost or the headaches of risk assessments!

Mathematics

Building in Second Life stealthily develops and practises maths skills. Building is a fun way to practise maths and a happy builder will barely notice either the amount of calculating required or their maths skills dramatically improving. Expert building and creation requires an understanding of coordinates, dimensions, angles and formulae. Coordinates and map-reading are also skills that can be introduced and developed in-world with challenges such as treasure hunts and orienteering tasks being easy to create.

Art & Design

Artists use the Second Life viewer's building tools to create simple or elaborate 3D sculptures and designs. Galleries can be easily erected and the students' work exhibited. Real-life images can be uploaded into Second Life and therefore students' real life art or graphics projects can also be displayed alongside their in-world designs and creations. In addition, the Second Life platform proves to be an incredibly economical, functional and manipulative environment for photography, video and Machinima projects. The content produced within Second Life is freely downloadable.

Drama

Second Life is an environment that supports the virtual planning of real-life productions and the production of in-world performances. From designing sets and experimenting with the placement of lighting, to costume design, sound effects and character movements, directors and actors can plan and rehearse most aspects of a show. The actors' performances and speech can either be controlled by pre-defined animations, gestures and media players or be 'acted' (produced) in real-time by the performers.

Computing

Scripts are used within Second Life to perform functions such as making objects speak, rotate or play sounds and also for more complex tasks such as powering vehicles, communicating with the wider Internet or handling payments. LSL (Linden Scripting Language), the language developed for Second Life, is a wonderfully simple introduction to computer programming and incorporated into the viewer is a helpful LSL script editor. Students can be introduced to variables, syntax and other programming skills by experimenting and changing simple aspects of the code within scripts and then observing the results.

Science

The Second Life platform can be imaginatively used to conduct stimulating experiments that are not normally possible or practical in a classroom. Objects can be easily modified to create unusual physical effects such as zero gravity. These novel environments and the experiments produced within them can be prepared cheaply and in advance, then repeated as often as required with little further effort and without further expense.

Media Studies

Newspapers, radio stations and even television stations can all be established in Second Life at little or no cost. With a multitude of residents using a technology at the forefront of inter-personal communications, I'm not sure I can imagine a more suitable environment for contemporary media studies, including the analysis of new media on the Internet, virtual worlds, and as the platform develops, the scope to explore and assess the impact of further connectivity using, for example, mobile devices, interactive television and other forms of mass media.

Irie note

It should be noted that the Second Life Grid is for adults only (18+). **Teen Second Life is the grid provided for 13–17-year-olds** (for details refer to the Teen Second Life website at http://teen.secondlife.com).

It's a business opportunity

The entrepreneurial economy of Second Life is driven by the facts that Second Life's Terms and Conditions grant to residents the intellectual property (IP) rights of their own creations and that Linden dollars are easily and legally exchangeable for US dollars. Content creators are therefore able to sell their goods to other residents, and other residents can be hired to provide an ever-increasing range of professional and personal services. Thousands of residents are now creating significant real-world incomes from their Second Life enterprises. These in-world ventures largely succeed due to the ingenuity, artistic ability, entrepreneurial acumen and developed reputation of their owners.

For existing businesses

Internal and external communications, marketing and retail have historically been at the forefront of corporate Internet activity and as a thriving social networking environment, it didn't take long for real-world businesses to exploit these existing opportunities on the Second Life platform and then to start to develop further opportunities and applications.

Second Life's 3D environment combined with both real-time voice and text communication provide businesses with the opportunity to offer a unique sense of presence and engagement to remote co-workers and distant customers alike. This permits almost limitless scope for businesses to test products, analyse business models, conduct market research, receive product feedback, recruit, train and maybe most excitingly to permit remote employees to collaborate on projects in 3D and in real-time. For example, a concept car can be produced in Second Life then the engineers from far-flung offices can walk around and examine the project discussing the design and its features. Second Life can then be used to ask what other residents (consumers) think of the design and whether it looks better like this or like that.

Real-world businesses currently find in-world success in marketing and building brand awareness by advertising, hosting in-world events and offering experiences and inducements to generate the interest of Second Life Residents. Relative to the real world, start-up and running costs in Second Life are inexpensive with the potential upside in market reach appearing quite staggering.

Many real-world businesses are already established on the Second Life grid:

+ Mazda launched their concept car Hakaze in-world.

+ Dell and Adidas both have in-world stores linking residents to real-world e-commerce systems where residents can purchase real products.

+ Coca-Cola hosted a premiere in Second Life that featured a performance by the pop singer Avril Lavigne.

+ F1 team IMG Renault have a free-to-use racing track both raising their brand awareness and serving as a fun source of information about the team and their sponsors.

These and numerous other forward-looking brands are building their in-world presence because they understand that in the not too distant future, tens of millions more consumers will shop and interact in-world. Imagine standing in your favourite department of a virtual music store, being able to see the other shoppers, discuss the recordings and interact with like-minded consumers. You don't have to imagine it; we have an iTunes outlet on our sim.

Charities and non-profit organizations

Charities, non-profit organizations and NGOs are utilizing Second Life by building in-world museums, libraries and facilities. The grid is a cost-effective and global platform for organizations to campaign and host events in order to both promote awareness and raise funds for their various causes. Second Life's non-profit programme allows qualifying members to benefit from discounted land rates.

Politics

Second Life offers rich possibilities for political campaigning and its resident ranks now include many professional politicians, their campaigns and the parties they belong to. Of course, political campaigning is not necessarily linked to party politics and it is issue-awareness that seems to generate more interest, action and debate amongst Second Life residents. Issues such as combating racism, building peace, fighting injustice, responding to disasters, etc. can be regularly, cheaply and immediately highlighted by concerned residents and groups.

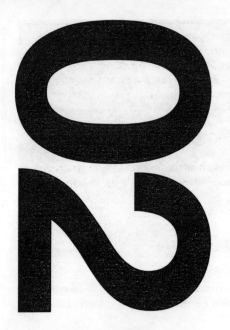

02

preparing for second life

In this chapter you will learn:

- how to check your computer's technical specifications
- to prepare your computer system for Second Life
- how to register an account and what to do before you log in

Please note that Irie Tsure's computer runs Windows XP and this chapter assumes that yours is the same. The Second Life viewer is available for the Windows Vista, Mac and Linux operating systems but you may need to refer to other literature for technical and optimization guidance.

Technical requirements

Running advanced software such as the Second Life viewer requires a certain threshold of computing power. Both the minimum and recommended requirements for the Second Life software can be found by clicking the **System Requirements** link at the bottom of the Second Life homepage (www.secondlife.com). If your system does not meet these minimum requirements, you are unlikely to be able to produce a workable, stable or enjoyable environment and Second Life may not even work at all.

Internet connection

A cable or DSL (Broadband) Internet connection is required to provide the necessary bandwidth for Second Life to operate. Bandwidth measures the rate at which data can be transferred through your Internet connection therefore the more bandwidth available the more quickly data can be transferred. A simple analogy to understanding bandwidth is to think of a hosepipe. The larger in diameter a hosepipe is, the more water can be pumped along it and in Internet terms the more bandwidth it provides.

Checking your Internet connection

Your agreement with your Internet service provider (ISP) will describe the type of service that your system is connected to. Second Life is not compatible with dial-up Internet, satellite Internet and some wireless Internet services.

Irie tip

You can do a precise check on your bandwidth using one of many free online bandwidth tools. Just type 'free bandwidth tool' or a similar phrase into your favourite search engine.

Central Processor Unit (CPU)

The Central Processing Unit (CPU) is the component within a computer system that executes programs. The power or speed of a CPU required to run the Second Life software depends upon the operating system but CPUs of less than 1GHz are likely to produce problematic in-world performance.

Memory (RAM)

RAM memory (not to be confused with other data storage devices like your hard disk) is the source of data directly accessed by your CPU. The more memory your computer has installed then the faster data can be accessed by the CPU and the better your Second Life experience becomes. The viewer requires a minimum of 512MB to operate but 1GB of memory or more is recommended for a better performance.

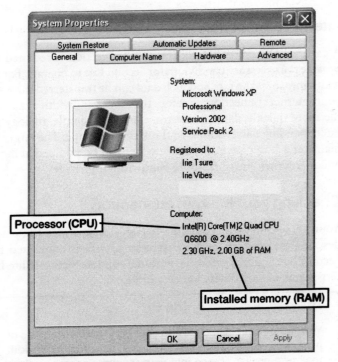

The Windows System Properties dialog box

Checking your CPU and RAM

To check your system's CPU and RAM, open the Windows Start menu, select the **Control Panel** and click the **System** icon (in future we will describe this progressive clicking as **Start > Control Panel > System**). You will find the system information under the General tab of the System Properties dialog box.

Graphics card

A graphics card, also referred to as a graphics accelerator card, display adapter or video card, generates and outputs images to your display. The more powerful the graphics card then the faster images can be created and the smoother and higher quality the resultant user experience. The Second Life viewer places great demands on graphics cards and may run incorrectly or not run at all on graphics cards other than the ones listed in the System Requirements. To identify which graphics card you have installed:

1 Select the **Hardware** tab on the **System Properties** dialog box.

2 Click on the **Device Manager** button.

3 Expand the view of Display adapters by clicking the adjacent plus sign.

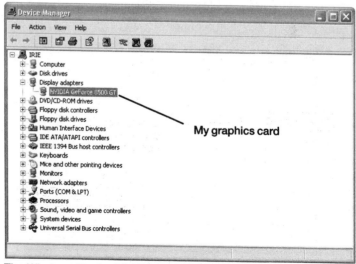

The Windows Device Manager

What a difference a powerful computer system makes!

I spent my first year in Second Life struggling with an old, slow and tired computer which barely scraped beyond the viewer's minimum requirements. This was often a frustrating experience particularly when operating in areas of Second Life well populated with other avatars and lots of objects. The CPU struggled to keep up with the flow of data coming from the Second Life servers and on regular occasions the viewer would freeze or crash (stop working or close) and it is very natural to blame Second Life for the jerky and unstable environment. But long-suffering residents inevitably adapt and develop a certain patience for such events (commonly referred to as *lag*).

It is only after an upgrade to a significantly more powerful system that one realizes these lag problems are caused almost exclusively *client side*, i.e. by the user's own system. Once I had upgraded to the system described below I discovered that Second Life is almost always a smooth, polished and incredibly stable platform even on the busiest of sims.

Irie Tsure's system

Internet Connection: DSL (Broadband)

Bandwidth: 3500 kbps

Computer memory RAM: 2GB DDR2

Operating System: Windows XP

Computer Processor: Intel Core 2 Quad x 2.4GHz

Graphics Card: NVIDIA Ge-Force 8500GT 1024 MB

I understand that powerful machines are not yet affordable for many Internet users but whatever system you have and subject to it reaching the minimum requirements, your Second Life experience will be smoother if your computer system is optimized for performance prior to installing the Second Life software.

Optimizing your system

Scan for viruses

A computer virus can severely affect your system's performance. Ensure that your antivirus software is regularly updated with the latest virus definitions and that you scan your system for viruses prior to installing the Second Life software and then at least once a week.

> ### Irie tip
> If you do not have up to date anti-virus software installed, you can scan your system for free and online either at:
>
> **http://housecall.trendmicro.com**
>
> or
>
> **http://onecare.live.com**

Clean the Registry

The **Registry** is a crucial part of your computer's operating system. Over time the registry will fragment and becomes cluttered with obsolete and unused data and this ultimately affects a computer's performance. You will find free registry cleaning software and free online registry scans by typing 'registry clean' or similar phrase into your preferred search engine. I use Microsoft's free 'Clean Up Scan' at http://onecare.live.com. Clean your registry prior to installing the Second Life software and then at least once a week to ensure you maintain optimum system performance.

Defrag the hard drive

With use and over time the data on a system's hard disk will fragment with files becoming scattered in pieces across its entirety. When a hard disk is fragmented your computer must search to find all the fragments of the files it needs and this process slows down a system's response time. Regularly defragmenting your hard disk helps your computer to access files more efficiently and therefore maintains optimum performance.

To defragment your hard disk:

1 Open (right-click > **Open**) the My Computer icon and right-click on the drive you wish to defrag (often the C: drive).

2 Select **Properties** from the drop-down menu and a Windows dialog box will appear.

3 Click on the **Tools** tab.

4 Click the **Defragment Now...** button.

5 Once the Disk Defragmenter opens, highlight the drive you wish to defragment.

6 Click the **Defragment** button.

Update the drivers

Your operating system (OS) cannot communicate directly with many of the devices that connect to your computer. Device drivers are therefore required to act as interpreters between the installed devices and the OS. For example the graphics card, the sound card and the monitor all require device drivers installed. Your OS already contains pre-installed drivers for many different devices connected to your system. These tend to be generic and often support only the basic features of the device being installed. You should always download and install the drivers created by the hardware manufacturer so that your OS can use all the device's features efficiently. Hardware manufacturers release new versions of their drivers to fix problems (bugs), increase performance, improve stability, add new features and take advantage of new OS features. As manufacturers release new drivers you must replace your existing drivers with the newer version to take advantage of any improved performance and enhancements.

Irie note

A **Patch** is a mini-upgrade to a driver containing and replacing only those parts that have been updated.

Using incorrect or out-dated device drivers hinders a computer's performance and I recommend that you take the time to check your system is operating with *all* the latest drivers installed for *all* your devices. A list of all the devices connected to your computer can be found by using the Windows Device Manager (see page 15).

Updating all your system's device drivers is a pretty big job so let us concentrate on the priority driver update for Second Life which is the device driver for the graphics card. You should have already indentified the manufacturer and model of your graphics card from the device manager and to run Second Life properly the graphics card should be manufactured by NVIDIA (www.nvidia.com), ATI (www.amd.com) or Intel (www.intel.com).

When developers release a driver a version number is assigned to it and each time a new update is released for this driver, the version (v) number is increased (e.g. v1.1 becomes v1.2). In this way you can determine if you have the latest version of the driver. If the manufacturer's version number is higher than yours then you know that there is a newer version available for download. To determine the version of your current driver:

1   Open the device manager (as described previously).

2   Click on the plus sign next to Display adapters.

3   Click on the device which you would like the update.

4   Right-click then select **Properties** to display the properties window for your device.

5   Click on the **Driver** tab in the top of this window.

6   Write down the details in the **Driver Version** line (e.g. 6.14.11.6921).

You should now have identified the name, model, and version number of your graphics card and driver.

To determine if there is a newer driver available we must visit our graphics card manufacturer's website then access the download centre by clicking the link on the homepage marked 'Download Drivers', 'Support' or similar. NVIDIA and ATI both feature a menu-driven web page to help you download and install the correct driver.

GET DRIVERS BY PRODUCT

Option 1: Manually find drivers for my NVIDIA products. RECOMMENDED   Help

Product Type: GeForce

Product Series: GeForce 8 Series

Operating System: Windows XP

Language: English (UK)

My graphics card details   Search

Option 2: Automatically find drivers for my NVIDIA products. PRERELEASE   Learn More

Graphics Drivers   Motherboard Drivers

Much easier!

The NVIDIA Driver Download Centre

Once you have inputted the details of your own graphics card
and OS you will be directed to the correct download web page
for your device. You will there find the appropriate driver's
download link, release notes and installation instructions. Com-
pare this driver's version number to that of the driver installed on
your system. If the available driver's version number is higher,
then an updated driver is available for your device.

Irie tip

If a newer driver is available read both the release notes
and installation instructions prior to downloading the
drivers and carefully follow these instructions when
downloading and installing the drivers.

Alternatively you may choose to utilize any automated system
provided by the manufacturer to find the correct driver such as
seen above in NVIDIA's Option 2.

NVIDIA, ATI and Intel device drivers are almost always installed
using a self-executing installation program (i.e. file ends in .EXE)
so you will only need to download the software (to your desktop
for simple location), double-click the icon, click **Run** and follow

the on-screen instructions. When the software has finished installing your system will usually prompt you to reboot. Once you have rebooted your computer system should be using the updated drivers.

Many drivers for devices other than graphics cards will also be updated using downloadable self-executing installation programs. However, some device drivers do not come as executable programs (i.e. the file does not end with .EXE) and you will need to install such drivers manually following the device manufacturer's instructions that will be found within the release notes accessible via the corresponding driver's download web page.

Irie tip

Create a system 'Restore Point' prior to installing any new device driver and if you then make a mistake when installing drivers or a new driver causes system problems you can simply use the 'System Restore' utility to remove the driver and undo all the changes that have been made. To access the System Restore utility click 'Start' on your Windows desktop, > **All Programs** > **Accessories** > **System Tools** > **System Restore**. On the Welcome screen then select either 'Create a restore point' or 'Restore my computer to an earlier time' depending on what you want to do. Click 'Next' and follow the on-screen instructions.

Registering an account

Your computer should now be optimized and we are ready to enter the Second Life world. First we need to register and create an account – a basic account is free. Visit the Second Life homepage at www.secondlife.com then click the Get Started button.

On the subsequent page you are given the opportunity to select a basic look for your avatar. Our example 'Everything Criss' opts to become a fairly neutral 'Boy Next Door'.

Naming your character

You cannot ever change your avatar's name so do think carefully before making this decision. As you can see you can enter your choice of first name but must select the last name from a drop-down menu. The available Second Life last names change over time as new last names are introduced while others are withdrawn. The effect is that if I meet another avatar with the last name 'Tsure', I can be confident they registered within a few months of my own registration date.

In this example our new resident has chosen the first name 'Everything'. This is a good name specifically as it is gender neutral. Our example avatar may be yet to decide the gender (if any!) of this avatar and you never know, the gender might change again at a later date! Had 'Sally' been chosen as a first name then this could potentially cause a few eyebrows to rise if Sally ever chooses to evolve into a 7ft muscleman. A gender neutral name will keep

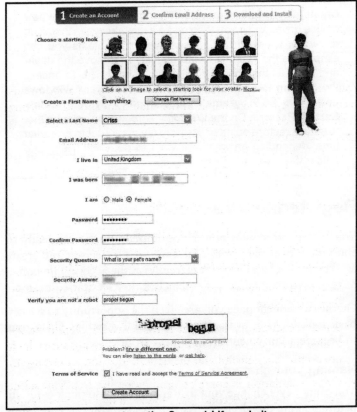

Registering an account on the Second Life website

your options open. Criss will be our example avatar's last name though he could have chosen a last name that more reflected his nationality or location.

Second Life names are unique and as such if you try to register a name that is already registered you will be asked to choose another. Inputting a date of birth and a valid email address as well as other required information such as gender, password and contact preferences completes this part of the registration process. Fill in this page as required, read and accept the terms of service then click **Create Account**.

Basic or premium account?

For now, unless you are absolutely certain that you will need to buy land immediately upon your arrival in Second Life, when you are asked whether you wish to upgrade to a Premium Account, click the **Skip this step** button. You can upgrade at any stage in the future should you decide to do so.

Your account is now created and all you need do to activate this account is to click on the link in the email that should be sitting in the inbox of the email address you provided a few moments ago. Once activated your web browser should automatically redirect to a download page. If not, there is a 'Download' link at the bottom of almost every page of the Second Life website.

Downloading the Second Life viewer

1 Click the download link then select **Run** (if you see a dialog box asking *'The publisher could not be verified. Are you sure you want to run this software?'* then click **Run** again).

2 Select your language, read the Release Notes if you want to, then click **Next**.

3 Select the directory into which the software should be installed then click the **Install** button. (If you are not sure which one to use, click **Install** and the default location will be used.)

4 Once installation is complete and assuming that you select **Yes** from the **Start Second Life Now?** dialog box, you should see a screen similar to this one.

The Second Life Viewer (see also Colour plate 1)

To log into the Second Life world you only now need to input your first name, last name and password then click the **Connect** button, but this screen also offers some information that you can, and in some cases that you should, be aware of prior to logging on.

Second Life Grid Status: When **Online** is displayed here then the Second Life grid is publicly accessible. When **Offline** is displayed here residents are unable to connect to Second Life and should try again later. The Second Life grid can be offline either due to scheduled maintenance or when a technical issue is causing grid-wide problems. Downtime on average equates to less than 1% of time (about seven hours per month).

Current Time: This is the universal time zone for the Second Life Grid and mirrors the current time in San Francisco, California (PST or PDT) where Linden Lab is based.

Logged In Last 60 Days: This is the total number of uniquely registered avatars that have logged into the Second Life grid during the previous 60 days.

Online Now: The total number of avatars currently logged into the Second Life grid.

Second Life Grid Status Reports: The latest Status Reports. Each title is a live link to a report like this one.

[Resolved] Logins disabled. In-world issues.

Posted by Status Desk on June 10th, 2008 at 02:58 pm PDT

[Resolved 3:18pm PDT] - Logins have been re-enabled and the database issue has been resolved. you can return to normal activities now.

Logins have been temporarily disabled to address the following:

We have identified a technical problem with our database. We are investigating and will keep you updated. This affects all in-world services. Please do not conduct transactions until we give an all clear.

This particular issue was quickly resolved but any resident logging on and being affected by this issue without checking this status report could have wasted a lot of time or worse lost money whilst trying to figure out what the problem was. The Status Report publishes information on current issues affecting the grid, their effects and gives progress reports. Read the Second Life Grid Status page before every log on and after every crash: http://status.secondlifegrid.net

News from the Official Second Life Blog: Visiting the Second Life Blog before every log on is a good habit that you should try to develop. When you click a Second Life Blog link you are shown a page featuring announcements, tips and information on new features.

You should by now have checked your system specifications, optimized your computer system and updated the device drivers as necessary. You've downloaded and installed the latest Second Life viewer and checked the Grid Status page for known issues. You have inputted your first name, last name and password into the Second Life viewer's welcome screen. You are now good to go and properly prepared to connect to the Second Life grid.

Click **Connect** now!

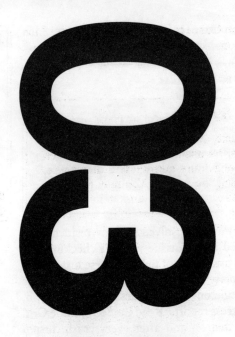

03 arriving in second life

In this chapter you will learn:

- what to expect when you arrive in-world
- how to communicate with other residents
- how to change your appearance

The first time you click the **Connect** button on the Second Life viewer you will be asked to accept the Second Life Terms of Service Agreement. You must agree and click 'Continue' in order to connect to the Second Life grid.

> ### Irie note
>
> Second Life has 'Community Standards', policies and policing prohibiting intolerance, harassment, assault and which clarify unacceptable behaviours surrounding disclosure, indecency and 'disturbing the peace'. You may receive a message posting these guidelines and it is wise to understand that ignoring these standards and policies may result in having your account suspended.

Pop-up dialog boxes (**pop-ups**) like this will periodically appear on screen to help with your orientation. Read these pop-ups as they appear then close them.

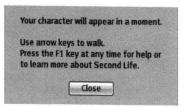

Your character will appear in a moment.

Use arrow keys to walk.
Press the F1 key at any time for help or to learn more about Second Life.

Close

Upon arrival

We first arrive in a region known as Orientation Island. We know this because all new avatars arrive here and also it states our current location in the top bar of the Second Life viewer. Our example avatar's first view of Second Life upon his arrival can be seen here. His name, *Everything Criss*, is visible for all to see above his head in the form of a *tag*.

In the top left corner of the viewer is the Second Life tutorial Heads Up Display (**HUD**). A HUD is only visible to you and detaches by right-clicking on it then selecting **Detach** from the pie menu that appears. You can either complete these in-world tutorials or detach the HUD and we can learn together all the skills (and many

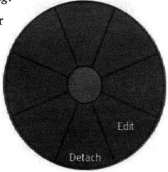

Edit

Detach

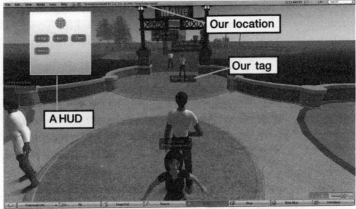

Our avatar's first view of the Second Life world (see also Colour plate 2)

more) described in these tutorials but in an order that I feel will be more conducive to your rapid development and rounded learning.

Irie tip

Do not concern yourself if you need to make interruptions during your reading of this chapter. Log off whenever you wish, for when you log back into the Second Life grid you will under normal conditions be returned to your last location, including here on Orientation Island. However I suggest you remain on Orientation Island until the end of this chapter as if you leave (except when logging off) then you will be unable to return here.

Moving your avatar

Use the up arrow on your keyboard to walk forward. This will put you in some space and avoid other avatars 'rezzing' on top of your head. Rezzing is the term commonly used to describe scenery, objects, textures and avatars appearing (*rendering*) in-world. You may have noticed when you logged on, depending on your system and the speed of your Internet connection, how the scene appeared to build up object by object. The faster your connection (the more bandwidth available) then the quicker the scene, the objects and other avatars will render.

Turn your avatar by using the left and right arrows on your keyboard and you should see four signs or areas marked Move, Search, Communicate and Appearance. These areas are learning opportunities and this is where the random nature of Second Life learning usual commences. The unguided newbie now walks towards the Appearance sign and starts to carve out their new identity. We see in the above image that three of the four other visible avatars have decided that their first priority is to be their appearance. We know this as '(Editing Appearance)' has appeared under their name tags and they have adopted an open standing stance. But let us take a moment to take on a more important issue; remember that you are on Orientation Island, that everybody is a newbie, so it matters not what you look like for a moment or two. Our priority is to ensure that when you venture further into Second Life, that with every movement, you start to appear as if you know what you are doing.

The random learning process common to most established residents is an incredible hindrance. Residents steer towards those Second Life skills that appear both quick and easy to master but remain intimidated by the skills that appear more difficult to grasp. This hampers our development individually and as a group. The irony is that much of what appears so complex in Second Life is in reality usually pretty simple. Order in the learning process will allow us to develop the skills required in Second Life without the 'that looks too complicated' gaps in our knowledge and also prevent residents falling from great heights into untidy heaps, i.e. the 'well I never knew that!' gaps.

For example: Press the [Home] key on your keyboard. You are flying! How cool! Press the [Page Up] key and you will ascend. Go as high as you can (about 200m) then press [Home] again. You just fell into that untidy heap I mentioned. Sorry about that, but better to make this most common of mistakes on Orientation Island than in the midst of a crowd that you are trying to impress. Pick yourself up, brush yourself off and press [Home] again. Again use [Page Up] to re-ascend. This time use [Page Down] to descend. Keep [Page Down] depressed until just after you land. Don't you agree that this is a far more stylish way to arrive?

Whether walking or flying the simplest method of moving your avatar is by using the up, down, left and right arrows on your keyboard. We can also depress the Up arrow and a Left or Right arrow to walk or fly in a left or right direction. Practise and experiment with your walking and flying skills by exploring Orientation Island.

Irie note

Using only your mouse to control avatar movement is managed by clicking **View** in the viewer's top menu and then selecting **Movement Controls** from the drop-down menu. An on-screen control panel will appear with which to move your avatar using your mouse.

As well as using [Home], your avatar will also start flying when you click the **Fly** button on either the on-screen Movement Controls (see note above) or on the viewer's bottom menu. Once clicked, **Fly** on the bottom menu changes to **Stop Flying**. Please remember that to descend from any altitude, using [Page Down] or the broken down arrow on the on-screen controller is infinitely preferable to the uncontrolled fall that will occur if the **Stop Flying** button or [Home] is employed.

The Mini-Map

Click on the **Mini-Map** button on the bottom bar to access the Mini-Map (keyboard shortcut [Ctrl] + [Shift] + [M]). This small map of the Sim we are currently on orientates to our avatar's position so we can deduce that our example avatar is currently facing north west. You are represented on your Mini-Map by the yellow dot. Other avatars at your altitude are indicated by green dots and avatars at a different altitude are indicated by the green arrowheads. The light triangle emanating from the yellow dot indicates the avatar's current camera view.

Moving the mouse cursor over the Mini-Map will reveal the name of the sim we are on and an option to open the main map (we will introduce this in due course). Right-clicking on the Mini-Map opens a menu to zoom close, medium and far (you can also zoom in and out on the Mini-Map by using a mouse scroll button if you have one).

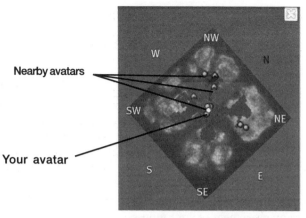

Nearby avatars

Your avatar

I almost always have the Mini-Map open in my viewer as it is the most unobtrusive way to keep an eye on the location and number of nearby avatars.

Looking around

The viewer's default camera position looks from just behind your avatar and as you turn, move or fly, the camera position and therefore your own view reflects your avatar's revised position and orientation. You can change the camera view in many ways including these most frequently useful controls:

- Press and hold down [**Alt**] on your keyboard ([**Option**] on a Mac) then clicking the **left mouse button** will focus the camera towards the surface you clicked on.

- [**Alt**] + click and hold the **left button** then dragging the mouse left and right will rotate the camera view around the surface you clicked on.

- [**Alt**] + click and hold the **left button** then dragging the mouse forwards and backwards will zoom the camera view towards and away from the surface you clicked on.

- [**Alt**] + [**Ctrl**] + click and hold the **left button** then dragging the mouse allows free camera control around and over the surface you clicked on.

- Pressing [**Esc**] restores the default camera view.

Mouselook

You can use your mouse to look around Second Life in a view best described as through your own avatar's eyes. Mouselook is useful when navigating within confined spaces such as beneath low ceilings that can interrupt the default camera view. It is also applied automatically when using some objects such as guns.

To enter Mouselook ensure that your chat bar is closed then press the [M] key. Alternatively, if your mouse has a scroll wheel then you can use it to zoom in until you enter Mouselook. To exit we can press [Esc] or use the mouse scroll to zoom out.

Once in Mouselook, your view from your avatar's position re-flects any movement of your mouse. The left, right, up and down arrow keys and [Page Up] and [Page Down] will now cause your avatar, and therefore your view, to move relative to the current view and not necessarily relative to your avatar (as in the default view). For example, if in Mouselook you are looking straight up, then pressing the up arrow would move your avatar (and view) towards your current view, i.e. straight up and not horizontally forward as would be the case using the default view.

Camera controls

Using only your mouse to control the camera view is managed by clicking **View** in the viewer's top menu and selecting **Camera Controls** from the drop-down menu.

The in-viewer camera control panel is displayed. This permits us to control our view using the mouse. This feature is very use-ful for the careful positioning of cameras when capturing images or recording video. **N.B.** the camera control cannot be accessed from Mouselook.

Communicating

On your travels around Orientation Island it is quite likely that you will see other new avatars. One may chat to you or you may wish to chat with another. When a nearby resident chats then you will see their name with their chat appearing from the lower left region of your viewer just above the bottom bar.

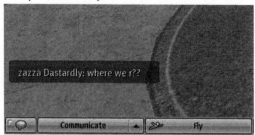

To start chatting just click the button or press [Enter] on your keyboard and the chat bar will appear just above the bottom menu bar of the Second Life viewer. Type into the text field provided, then broadcast your chat locally by pressing [Enter] or by clicking the **Say** button on the chat bar. By locally we mean that your chat will appear to other avatars within about a ten-metre radius of your avatar's position. You will also see any chat broadcast locally from other avatars within this range.

If you wish to broadcast your chat further than ten metres you would use the **Shout** command found by clicking on the little up arrowhead (▲) on the chat bar to the right of the **Say** button. Once clicked, a drop-down menu will be displayed where you will find the **Shout** command. Selecting Shout will broadcast your chat to all avatars within a radius of about 100 metres so this command should be used sparingly and only within appropriate environments.

Alternatively we can conduct our chat session within the **Communicate** window. We can display or hide (toggle) the Communicate window using the keyboard shortcut [Ctrl] + [H] or by clicking the **Communicate** button on the bottom menu bar. We can also access the Communicate window via the top menu bar: **View > Chat History**.

Irie tip

You can reposition windows within the Second Life viewer by clicking and holding down the left mouse button on the window's title bar while dragging the window to where you want it repositioned. You can also resize the Communicate and some other windows by clicking, holding then dragging the window's edge or corner.

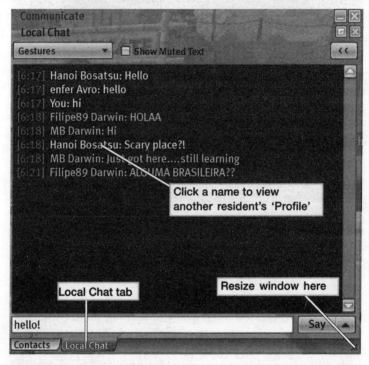

The Communicate window

When the Local Chat tab of the Communicate window is selected, the local chat history is displayed and everything that is said within about ten metres appears here instead of within the Second Life viewer window.

A new flashing tab suddenly appears to the right of the Local Chat tab. The avatar 'Filipe89 Darwin' has sent an Instant Message (IM) to our example avatar. Our avatar responds by select-

ing this new tab and typing a reply into the chat field then either
pressing [Enter] on the keyboard or by clicking the Send button.

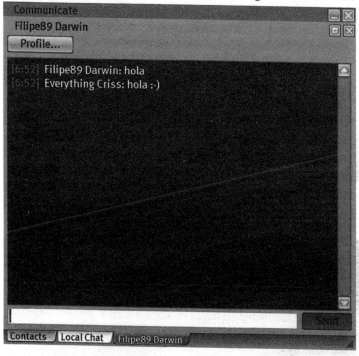

An Instant Message (IM)

To send your own IM to a nearby
avatar, right-click on the avatar
or their name tag to access this
pie menu.

Move the cursor over the pie-
menu to highlight **Send IM...** then
left-click to select. This opens a
new IM tab within the Communicate window. The avatar's
name appears on this tab and any
chat you have with this avatar

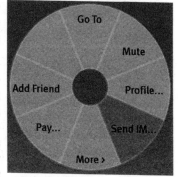

appears within both your Communicate windows but is not visible to the wider community.

Making friends

Once you engage in a conversation with someone that you might like to meet again, it may be an idea to ask them if you may add them to your friends list (it is considered polite to ask first). Friends by default automatically send each other a notification when they either log on or off so this is a most useful feature to keep a track of the comings and goings of the residents we meet. To send a friendship invitation, right-click their avatar to access their pie menu then select **Add Friend**. When I offered friendship to our example avatar he received the following pop-up:

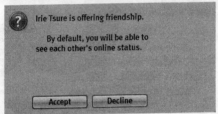

Once our avatar accepts my invitation I am notified that I have been added to his Friends list. We access our friends list by clicking on the **Contacts** tab of the Communicate window or by employing the keyboard shortcut [Ctrl] + [Shift] + [F].

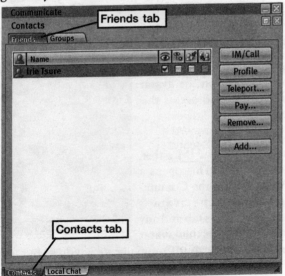

Friends list

You can also IM residents from your friends list by highlighting a friend's name then clicking the 'IM/Call' button.

Irie tip

Residents can IM up to 20 friends simultaneously in a Conference Chat. Prior to clicking the 'IM/Call' button, highlight additional friends to include in the conference chat by holding down [Ctrl] when selecting them one at a time with a mouse click.

We can view any friend's profile from our friends list by selecting their name then clicking the **Profile** button. An avatar's profile is a window that displays information about that avatar. Some information (e.g. the date a resident enters Second Life) is predetermined, but much of an individual's profile is self-edited and as such profiles can be used to gather some insight into who you meet. Obviously, on Orientation Island most avatars you meet will not yet have contributed to their profile. The **Contacts** tab also holds your Group list. We will come to groups in Chapter 6.

Irie tip

By default you will be logged out of the Second Life grid when you are inactive or away from your keyboard (AFK) for too long (approximately 10 minutes). This can become a real nuisance especially if you are working or learning from another window or application. To avoid disconnection from the grid, press [Ctrl] + [Alt] + [D] to display the Advanced menu within the viewer's top menu bar. Then from the top menu bar select **Advanced > Character > Character Tests > Uncheck Go Away/AFK When Idle** and you will never be logged out from Second Life for inactivity again.

Changing your appearance

Creativity within Second Life is initially and most commonly expressed in the form of avatar appearance. We have already remarked that the first thing the majority of people arriving in-world do is to change their appearance. You may have also noticed that in Colour plate 1, three of the visible avatars, like our example avatar, elected *Boy Next Door* as their basic avatar shape. Extremely unsatisfactory! All residents of Second Life quickly become familiar with these default avatar forms and it's a very easy way to identify newbies as they wander across the grid.

Of course it is important to stamp your identity on your avatar but it is not important to get it perfect first time. Avatars evolve over time and we can change our look at any time. But let us make a start.

Use the Mini-Map (keyboard shortcut [Ctrl] + [Shift] + [M]) to find a nice quiet space then access the **Appearance** menu by right-clicking on your avatar then choosing **Appearance** from the pie menu. (This can also be accessed through the top menu **Edit >**

The Appearance menu

Appearance.) Your avatar will adopt an open standing stance, 'Editing Appearance' is displayed in your tag and the Appearance menu is opened (see above).

Whilst in appearance mode it is often helpful to change the camera view using the following controls:

* [Alt] + click and hold the **left button** then dragging the mouse left and right will rotate the camera view around your avatar.

* [Alt] + click and hold the **left button** then dragging the mouse forwards and backwards will zoom the camera view towards and away from your avatar

* [Alt] + [Ctrl] + click and hold the **left button** then dragging the mouse allows free camera control around and over your avatar.

To change our avatar's appearance we explore and experiment with the different settings within the **Body Parts** section of the Appearance window:

From the **Shape** tab we may change our avatar's gender by selecting either the **Male** or **Female** radio button.

When the **Body** button (from the **Shape** tab) is selected we can adjust our avatar's height, body thickness and body fat by using the slider controls displayed. Adjustments are applied immediately to the avatar and the slider panels illustrate the setting extremes. Within the **Shape** tab we may also adjust the many different settings for our avatar's head, eyes, ears, nose, mouth, chin, torso and legs.

We can inflict random appearance variations on our avatar by clicking on the **Randomize** button. Click it again and again. When we are finished experimenting with Randomize feature we will probably click the **Revert** button. This will undo all changes made since the avatar's appearance settings were last saved. In our example, and as we are yet to save any specific appearance, our avatar would revert to the default appearance of the Boy Next Door.

Adjusting the settings within the **Skin** tab determines your avatar's skin colour, skin details, makeup and body detailing.

The **Hair** tab determines the colour and style of your hair, eyebrows and facial hair.

The **Eyes** tab changes your eye colour, eye lightness and (in due course and if you wish) where you can change the image file for your eyes.

Residents use these tabs and sliders to create our unique and wonderful appearances. However you do not need to achieve any kind of perfection at this stage as further adjustments can be made at any time. Once you are reasonably happy with the basis of your new look click **Save** then **Close**.

An introduction to the inventory

The *inventory* is where residents keep their Second Life possessions. You already have hundreds of items in your own inventory. Access the inventory window by clicking the **Inventory** button in the Second Life viewer's bottom menu bar or by using the keyboard shortcut [**Ctrl**] + [**I**].

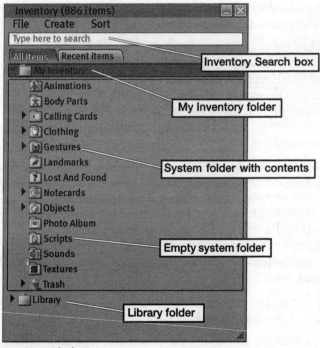

The Inventory window

Irie note

Details of the items in your inventory are stored on Second Life servers therefore your inventory may sometimes take as long as a few minutes to fetch or display all the items held within it.

Our example avatar has arrived into Second Life with 886 items already in his inventory! We know this because we can see the total displayed within the Inventory title bar.

By default the **All Items** tab is displayed and therefore we can see a list of all the folders within the inventory. Our in-world possessions are contained within these conveniently categorized folders. The contents of folders with an arrow (▶) to the left are hidden and the folder is opened and the contents displayed by clicking on the arrow. Folders without an arrow are currently empty.

The inventory is divided into two main sections; *My Inventory*, where you keep your own items and *Library* where Second Life's stock items are stored. Library items are accessible to all residents and the library is stocked by Linden Lab. Therefore you cannot save your own items to the Library section of the inventory. Simple icons are used to represent different types of items in your inventory.

Irie tip

You can create sub-folders inside your inventory folders to further categorize your possessions. From the title bar of the Inventory window select **Create > New Folder**. To rename the new folder, right-click on the folder then select Rename from the drop-down menu.

N.B. Residents cannot rename system folders such as the *Clothing* or *Body Parts* folders. All system folders are marked with an appropriate icon.

Clothing

Blue jeans and white T-shirt are not quite the fashion statement our example avatar wants to make but very kindly Linden Lab has supplied us with some wardrobe options within the Library section of the inventory.

1 Click the ▼ adjacent to **My Inventory** to hide its contents.

2 Open the *Library* folder by clicking the adjacent ▶.

3 Within the Library folder, open the *Clothing* folder by clicking on the adjacent ▶.

Within the Library's clothing folder you will find further folders containing entire wardrobes of clothes. Open one of these folders and/or scroll down a little and you will start to see your available garments.

To wear an item of clothing listed in the inventory:

1 Click on the inventory item then hold down the left button and drag the item onto your avatar, then release the button.

Or

2 Right-click on the item in your inventory then select **Wear** from the drop-down menu.

Either way the new item of clothing will replace any equivalent item of clothing previously worn by our avatar.

To remove an item of clothing:

1 Right-click on the item in your inventory then select **Take Off** from the drop-down menu.

Or

2 Right-click on your avatar then select **Take Off > Clothes >** (e.g.) **Shirt** from the pie menu.

Irie tip

To most quickly identify and group all the items your avatar is wearing, enter the search-term **'worn'** into the Inventory search box.

Take some time to explore your inventory and try on some different clothing items. Once you have settled on both your appearance and your clothing you will have in front of you, your very first Second Life creation. Remember that you can change any aspect of your appearance at any time and that you will acquire lots more clothing as you progress, so for now, please don't fret if your avatar is not yet the supermodel you envisaged. **Save All** then **Close** the Appearance window.

Everything Criss

Our example avatar (AKA a typical newbie)

We are very nearly ready to leave our orientation. Just a couple more things you ought to be aware of. Within the Second Life viewer's top menu bar you will see the in-world clock, your money and a search box (we will learn all about search in the next chapter).

12:01 AM PST   L$0   Search

Second Life time

Second Life is a global community with residents operating in all the world's time-zones. To avoid the obvious confusion that would be wrought by all residents referring to their local time and because Linden Lab are situated in San Francisco, in-world clocks display Pacific Time; which is PST or PDT depending on the time of year.

Money

Your avatar's in-world balance is displayed in Linden dollars (L$) to the right of the in-world clock. Our example avatar has no money, but at present this is not a problem. If you do require money immediately you will need to purchase L$s (see page 81). But do not rush for your credit card for in the next chapter we discuss how to acquire everything you will need for now (including some money) for free!

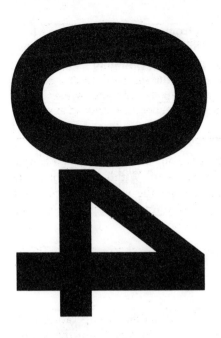

04

**exploring
second life**

In this chapter you will learn:

- how to interact with objects
- how to navigate and teleport around the Second Life grid
- how to search Second Life for the things you want

We are now ready to move on from our orientation. But where to go?! Our example avatar is diligent and when he comes across a 'Visit Help Island!' sign, as per the suggestion to 'Just click this sign for a landmark', he left-clicks the sign.

Irie note

When our example avatar touches this sign, he triggers an event that in turn calls a pre-programmed and specific function, i.e. this sign obeys the following command – 'In the event that I am touched by an avatar then I will perform the function of delivering a Landmark to that avatar.'

Interacting with objects

Left-click first!!

In this example the sign's creator has assigned a Touch event to the left-click so that when the sign is left-clicked (*touched*), the object will perform the functions the creator intended.

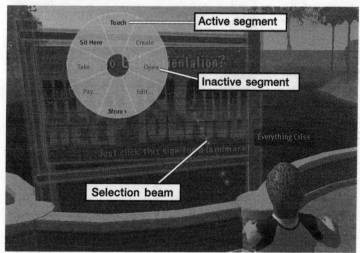

Selecting by right-clicking on an object

Right-clicking on the sign will instead select the object and a selection beam as well as a pie menu will be displayed. In this example, when the object is right-clicked, the **Touch, Sit Here** and **More>** segments of the pie menu are bold, clearly visible and therefore these actions are available to be selected. The other segments, i.e. **Create, Open, Edit, Pay** and **Take,** are inactive and as such these actions cannot be selected for this object.

We don't want to sit on the sign (although we can if we want to) so the most reasonable segment to select is **Touch.** The creator intended the sign to perform a function when touched and scripted the object accordingly. But touching the sign was always achieved more simply by left-clicking this object. So it is better to initially left-click an object in order to see what function it is designed to perform.

Two functions are triggered by the sign when our avatar touches the sign (either by left-clicking on it or by **right-click > Touch**). The sign's first function is to say: *'Visit Help Island, Click for Landmark: Everything, a landmark window just opened on your screen. Click the 'Teleport' button to travel to Help Island where volunteers are waiting to assist you. Please note you will be unable to return to this Orientation Island.'*

Objects as well as avatars can chat and the sign's speech is displayed as chat in the main window of the Second Life viewer.

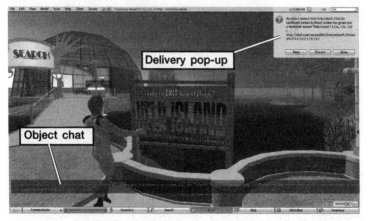

Actually, a Landmark window did not appear in our avatar's viewer but what does appear is a pop-up asking him whether he wishes to accept the item that the sign is attempting to deliver (the second function).

Irie warning!

Beware of accepting items from unfamiliar objects or avatars. Read the delivery pop-up carefully as to where and who the item is being delivered from and what the item is. Do you want this item? Do you trust the source? There are instances of some residents delivering malicious items and causing problems for residents! If you either don't want the item or are unsure of its pedigree then click the **Discard** button. Discarding the item will not prevent its delivery to your inventory but instead place the object in your Inventory Trash folder from where it can be purged or restored later should you wish to delete or retrieve it.

Our example avatar clicks on the delivery pop-up's **Keep** button. The Help Island landmark is then delivered to the *Landmarks* folder within his inventory and also opens in the viewer.

Landmarks (LM)

A Second Life landmark (an LM) acts as a bookmark or favourite for an in-world location by recording and displaying the parcel name, the region name and a position on the region to the nearest metre in the form of X,Y and Z coordinates. A landmark also can and often does, display a description of the parcel and an accompanying image. The primary purposes of landmarks are to facilitate exploring and to permit simple navigation between a resident's favourite locations.

We can create landmarks at any time from the viewer's top menu **World > Create Landmark Here** and the new landmark will be created within the *Landmarks* folder. However, if you try to create a landmark on Orientation island you will get the message 'You cannot create a landmark here...' This is because some areas do not allow landmarks to be created in order to prevent residents from returning there without invitation.

Name: 'Irie Vibes' Caribbean Reggae Music Nightclub Resort & Shoppin
Description:

'Irie Vibes' Reggae Music Resort, Irie (154, 156, 27)

Information: Traffic: 20879 Area: 62720 sq. m.
Location: Irie 154, 156, 27 (PG)

Teleport   Show on Map

A landmark

There are three simple ways to visit or **teleport** (**TP**) to a landmark:

- Double-click a landmark in your *Landmarks* folder.

- Right-click a landmark in your *Landmarks* folder then select **Teleport** from the drop-down menu.

- Right-click on the landmark in your inventory then select **About Landmark** from the drop-down menu. This will open a landmark and we teleport by clicking the **Teleport** button.

When you teleport you will experience a Teleporting... screen. This screen may appear for a split second or up to a minute depending on how quickly your teleport can be arranged. When you arrive and if you're not precisely at the landmark's coordinates then a red beacon with a red arrow will indicate the exact landmark location and display your distance from it.

Irie tip

Even long-term residents rarely realize that we can left-click this red arrow to make it and the red beacon disappear.

A note of where you have just teleported from appears in your chat window. This message will only be visible to you. This is an extremely useful feature as it permits you to quickly return from whence you came in the event of any kind of unfortunate or embarrassing teleporting incident. To return, simply (and usually rapidly) click on the Second Life location-reflecting link in the chat text. This class of link is referred to as a *SLurl* (see page 63).

Once our example avatar has teleported to Help Island he finds several interesting areas. Our avatar first visits the:

Demo area

In the Demo area our avatar finds the opportunity to examine and use some of the objects created by Second Life employees and residents. Our avatar finds a show home and upon entry discovers some pose-ball furniture.

Pose-balls

Pose-balls are spheres that trigger animations in our avatars. The pose-balls in our example all have 'Sit' displayed above them in what is termed as *floating text*.

Irie note

Left-clicking these (and many other) pose-balls seems to achieve nothing. Though creators can assign a Sit function to the left-click event of a pose-ball it is uncommon as they often use the Touch event to hide (make transparent) their own pose-balls.

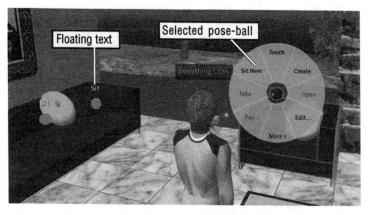

Our avatar right-clicks a pose-ball then selects the 'Sit Here' option from the pie menu.

The pose-ball takes control of our avatar, positions and rotates him as necessary then places him in the pose or animation the creator of the pose-ball has programmed. We can no longer move our avatar; the up, down, left and right arrows on the keyboard now serve to control the camera view and at present do not control the avatar.

Once rested and when he wants to continue his exploring we click the 'Stand Up' button and our normal movement controls are regained.

Pose-balls are used in Second Life for a multitude of purposes including but not limited to dance animations, poses and animations for furniture and all sorts of couple/group animations. Pose-balls that trigger gender specific poses or animations are often coloured pink and blue accordingly.

Irie tip

Remember to left-click objects as you explore. By left-clicking on objects around this room, our avatar soon discovers a wall-switch by the door that controls some very cool window blinds.

Notecards

Exploring Help Island introduces us to many tutorials, guides and video tutorials. These tutorials are often contained as notecards within objects. Touch (left-click) a tutorial object and a notecard will be delivered to your inventory in the same way as we described when acquiring the Help Island landmark. Notecards can be accessed in the **My Inventory > Notecards** folder. To open a notecard from your inventory either double-click on the notecard or right-click > **Open** the notecard.

Irie note

Though our avatar diligently collects all the notecards from this area, he has a copy of this book, so doesn't attempt any of these tutorials just now.

Freebie Store

Moving on, our avatar is greeted by a Freebie Store and I suggest that you partake in some enthusiastic shopping here. To collect free items go inside the store, browse then left-click the items you wish to take. Objects that deliver items to residents, free or otherwise, are referred to as *vendors*. Often you will see a delivery pop-up in the same way as previously described with landmarks and the notecards. Clicking **Keep** on the pop-up delivers the item to your inventory. This method of delivery is designed so that upon the vendor being touched, a copy of the freebie item is delivered to the touching avatar's inventory.

Sometimes the freebie item must be bought from the vendor. The creator of such a vendor has assigned a **Buy** event to the left-click rather than the touch event previously described. When this type of vendor is left-clicked, a **Buy Contents** window appears. Within this window the items on offer are visible.

Resize this window or scroll down to examine all the contents. Details of both the retailer and the cost are displayed underneath these contents. There is also a check box offering the option to 'Wear clothing now'. In this case our example avatar is buying dance animations and therefore the option to wear, though visible, is not available for selection.

If you want to buy the items then click the **Buy** button and the item or items will be delivered to a folder in your inventory. If you don't wish to proceed, then select the **Cancel** button.

Irie warning!

Using the 'Wear clothing now' option in a public place can prove horribly embarrassing. As clothes rez on your avatar they may appear transparent during some of the process and furthermore if the clothes are not quite the size or the fit that you expect then further embarrassment may also be experienced. I strongly recommend finding a nice quiet spot to try on or change into clothes.

Our example avatar collects almost every freebie available to him. I suggest you do the same as there is currently no limit to the amount of items that we can store within an inventory. Your inventory will inevitably and rapidly increase in size and therefore we will discuss several methods to effectively manage an overflowing inventory in Chapter 5. But for the moment grab everything that is even vaguely interesting!

Locating new items in the inventory

To find your most recent acquisitions open the inventory either by selecting the **Inventory** button on the bottom menu or with the keyboard shortcut [**Ctrl**] + [**I**].

Select the **Recent Items** tab to filter your inventory to (by default) display only the items you have received since your last log off. In our avatar's example only those collected from tutorial vendors and freebie vendors are displayed.

Selecting **File** > **Show Filters** from the inventory window's menubar opens a further window. This **Filters** window allows for specific groups of items to be either included or excluded in the displayed results. By selecting **Since Logoff** only those items received into inventory since the avatar's previous logoff are displayed and this is a very useful feature when it comes to quickly locating items that have been recently acquired. These filters can be independently applied to both the inventory's **All Items** tab and the **Recent Items** tab.

Our avatar sets the filter for the **Recent Items** tab to display all items received since logoff and only those folders containing newly acquired freebies and notecards are displayed. He then clicks the

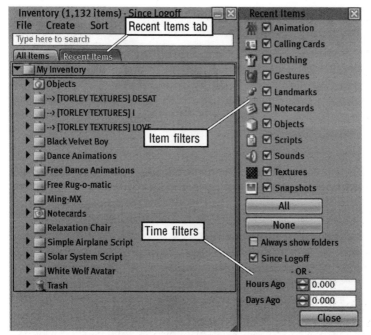

▶ adjacent to the folder he wishes to expand in order to display the folder's contents. Single item purchases are delivered to the *Objects* folder while multiple item purchases such as the Dance Animations will have created their own folder within the inventory.

Collecting some freebies inspires our avatar to evolve his appearance. The *White Wolf Avatar* folder has caught his eye and he selects the entire *White Wolf Avatar* folder by holding down the left button then drags the folder onto his avatar. All wearable contents of this folder are applied to our avatar and over the next few seconds he transforms into a handsome white wolf.

The Sandbox

Not all the items in the inventory should be worn of course. To render the freebie Relaxation Chair for example, our avatar will need to drag the object from the inventory and onto the ground. However, many parcels will not permit just any old avatar to render objects as this would undoubtedly lead to huge amounts of littering and parcel owners would spend large chunks of each

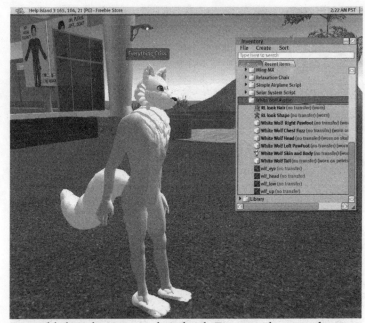

in-world day clearing up their land. Fortunately, some benevolent landowners do permit residents to render objects on designated land parcels for the purposes of accessing inventory items, practice, learning and creativity. Such an area is referred to as a public sandbox. Help Island has a public sandbox and in this area we can render our objects in order to use or examine them more closely. We render an object by dragging the object from our inventory and onto the ground.

Irie note

We can only render objects in-world and not inventory items such as textures, animations, clothing items, etc.

Search

It is important to take some time to explore Second Life and to have some fun. Next to your L$ balance and the in-world clock is a search box. Type something in the search box. Try 'free', 'nightclub', 'garden', 'beach', 'funfair', etc. Our example avatar can be more specific, he knows precisely where he wants to party and when he types the search-term 'irie' into the search box the following **Search Second Life** window appears.

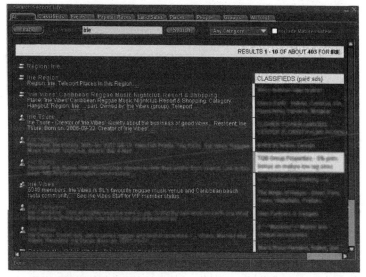

Search Second Life window

By default the **All** tab of the Search Second Life window is opened and the displayed results include the places, events, residents and groups most relevant to our search term. Paid classified advertisements are displayed down the right-hand side of the window.

Those who use the Google search engine will find the Second Life search layout extremely familiar as the search functionality is powered by a Google engine. It therefore supports both Boolean logic and phrase searching as well as keyword searching.

Boolean logic refers to a search term in which the words AND, NOT (represented by '–') and OR are used to refine a search. This can be very useful when constructing a search term for specifying exactly the information you require.

Boolean logic search term examples

AND: We are searching for male skin:

Search term: male skin (**N.B.** the 'AND' is implied and need not be included)

NOT: We are looking for live music, but not country!

Search term: live music –country (**N.B.** 'NOT' is represented by '–')

OR: We are looking for cats or dogs

Search term: cats OR dogs

Phrase searching refers to when we are looking for results that include an exact phrase. To search for a phrase just put quotation marks around your search term.

Phrase searching example

We are looking for a particular resident named "Everything Criss"

Search term: "Everything Criss"

The Search Second Life window also has other tabs to allow for searches within specific categories.

- **Classifieds:** To search only within residents' classified advertisements.

- **Events:** To search Second Life events running currently or starting soon.

- **Showcase:** To display Second Life's most popular venues.

- **Land Sales:** To find land for sale or rent.

- **Places:** To search land parcels.

- **People:** To search for a resident.

- **Groups:** To search for a group.

The Search Second Life window can be accessed at any time by selecting the **Search** button on the bottom menu bar or by [**Ctrl**] + [**F**] (for Find) on the keyboard. Our example avatar selects 'Irie Vibes' from the search results and the conclusion of the search is displayed.

This search conclusion window offers us a description of our chosen venue, often a picture, the parcel category (e.g. hangout, shopping, etc.), the region in which the place is located, the owner, a teleport button and a list of the objects for sale on the parcel.

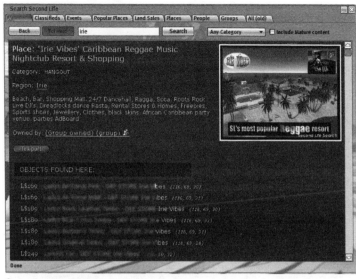

Search conclusion

Our avatar teleports to the 'Irie Vibes' reggae resort, uses his Mini-Map to find the crowd, joins the party then gets his groove on. It has been a busy day of learning and he wants to make some friends.

A regular good night out is a Second Life requirement

Irie tip

When in a busy venue I have found the most effective method to simultaneously keep up with both IMs and broadcast chat is to tick the 'Show chat bubbles' checkbox found on the 'Text Chat' tab of the Preferences window ([Ctrl] + [P]). When I zoom back from my avatar I can then use the Communicate window exclusively for IMing with friends (or for being teased by that Zib Scaggs) but can also keep a vague eye on the chat broadcast by nearby residents.

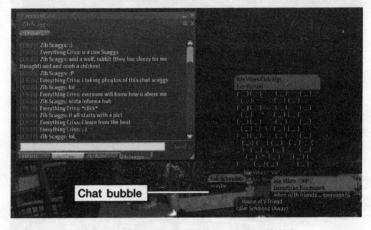

Chat bubble

Trying to keep up with both Chat and IMs can be tricky!

The World Map

The World Map is used by residents to navigate and explore the Second Life grid. From the World Map we can teleport to any public parcel, track friends, locate crowds and identify land for sale or auction. We display the World Map either by clicking the **Map** button in the viewer's bottom menu bar or from the top menu bar **View > World Map** or by using the keyboard shortcut [Ctrl] + [M].

By left-clicking and holding down the mouse button anywhere on the World Map we can drag the map view. We can also zoom in and out of our view of the map by either using the Zoom slider control or with the scroll wheel on our mouse (if we have one).

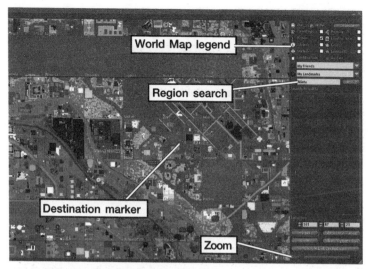

The World Map (see also Colour plate 3)

The World Map legend allows residents to locate several categories of potential interest such as other avatars, an Infohub and ongoing Second Life events. We hide or display these categories of interest by ticking or un-ticking the corresponding checkboxes.

You: This icon indicates your current location on the Second Life grid.

Home: A blue house indicates your Home location (see **Infohub**).

Classifieds: This indicates the locations of Classifieds listings.

Person: The green dots indicate the locations of other avatars.

Infohub: This indicates the location of an Infohub (or Welcome Area). This is an entry or gathering point on the Second Life Grid. The first Infohub you landed at after completing your orientation automatically gets set as your home location. You can set any Infohub to be your Home location via the Second Life viewer's top menu bar: **World > Set Home to Here.**

Telehub: This icon indicates the location of a Telehub. A Telehub is an object acting as a parcel's landing point.

Land For Sale: The $ icon indicates the location and displays the cost of land parcels for public sale.

Events: The pink star icon indicates the locations of PG-rated in-world events.

Events (M): The blue star icon indicates the locations of Mature rated in-world events.

Land For Sale: Yellow areas on the World Map indicate the position, size and shape of land parcels that are for public sale.

Auction: Purple areas on the World Map indicate the position, size and shape of land parcels that are set for sale by public auction.

Destination markers

When a destination is set (e.g. by left-clicking on a valid location on the World Map) it is indicated as a red circle. A vertical red beacon and a red arrow also appear as markers within the viewer to guide us towards our destination. We clear these markers by clicking the **Clear** button on the World Map or with a left-click on the red arrow destination marker visible within the viewer.

Other functions

To further assist residents in their navigation and exploration of the Second Life grid, the World Map has other useful functions.

My Friends

Residents can use the World Map to track each other across the Second Life grid.

Irie note

Residents must grant their friends permission to locate them in-world before they can be tracked using the World Map. This is managed via the Friends list ([Ctrl] + [Shift] + [F]). To let someone locate you on the World Map, select their name on your Friends list then tick the appropriate checkbox under the 'Friend can locate you on the map' icon.

With a left-click, select a friend from the World Map 'My Friends' drop-down menu. If your friend is online then the destination markers will appear indicating their in-world location.

My Landmarks

The My Landmarks drop-down box displays a list of all the landmarks in your inventory. Select a landmark with a left-click and its destination markers will appear.

Region search

Residents can use the World Map to search for a region by typing part of or its entire name into the region search field then pressing the **Search** button. The search results will display any matching regions. Select a region with a left-click and its destination markers will appear.

Teleporting

Residents can attempt to teleport to any location on the Second Life grid simply by selecting a valid destination on the World Map then pressing the **Teleport** button. It is possible, due to a telehub, technical issues or parcel restrictions, that you may not teleport to precisely the location you instructed. The in-world destination markers are there to guide you the rest of the way.

Copy SLurl to Clipboard

Pressing the **Copy SLurl to clipboard** button copies a SLurl of a selected destination to your system's clipboard.

SLurls

SLurls, much like landmarks, serve to act as 3D bookmarks to in-world locations, however, unlike Landmarks, SLurls are useable from both inside and outside Second Life. They can therefore be used not only for posting Second Life locations in-world but also, for example, on web pages and within blogs or emails.

A SLurl providing a direct link to a location in Second Life typically includes the name of a region along with three coordinates and looks like this:

http://slurl.com/secondlife/Irie/144/131/37.

Paste a SLurl into a web browser's address bar. A map will be displayed and the SLurl location will be indicated. Assuming that a user has the Second Life viewer installed, clicking on the **Teleport now** button will automatically open their Second Life viewer and teleport them directly to the SLurl location in-world.

Finding free stuff

Wherever your explorations take you it is quite likely that you will find stores. At this time there really is no good reason for the newbie to spend any money at all because the grid is strewn with *freebies*. These most commonly are objects that other residents have created and are happy to share with the wider community or are being offered as an inducement to visit a particular parcel. Type 'free', 'freebie', 'free stuff' or similar terms into the search box and accumulate as many free items as you possibly can. There is currently no limit to the amount of items you can store in your inventory and in Chapter 5 we discuss ways to manage a growing inventory. At present just find the time to visit parcels offering freebies and collect almost everything you find.

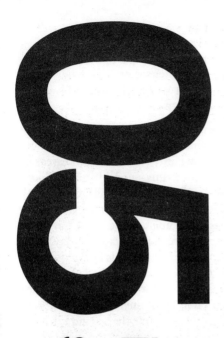

05

interacting in second life

In this chapter you will learn:

- more about interacting with objects
- how to shop and manage your inventory
- how to access in-world music and video
- how to record pictures and video

Lag and your system

The Second Life viewer is a cutting edge application which will test the limits of much of your computer system. Your video card, CPU and your Internet connection will all be incredibly active while you explore the Second Life grid.

On your initial travels and depending on the technical specifications of your computer, you will almost certainly have experienced differing levels of performance when visiting different areas of the grid. In some regions the viewer runs smoothly almost like a movie whilst in other places your avatar almost grinds to a halt and the viewer experience is jerky, unstable and may crash altogether. You will hear residents screaming in frustration 'Lag! Lag! This sim is SO LAGGY!' or 'Second Life is laggy today. Why don't the Lindens just sort it out?!'. In reality this is like riding up the motorway on a bicycle then complaining that we are not travelling at 100mph. These residents do not understand that they are actually stating that their system, be it their computer or their Internet connection, is just not up to running the Second Life software at an acceptable level and the resultant experience is frustrating them.

I understand the frustration of this particular situation all too well. We can't all afford the latest and most powerful computers. My first year in Second Life was experienced using a Pentium 4 processor that under most circumstances just wasn't up to delivering a smooth experience. But needs must and like many, many residents I developed that 'Second Life patience' for the experiences that are commonly known as lag, freezing and crashing.

What is lag?

Lag most commonly refers to any slowdown or interruption in flow experienced by a resident, be it low frame-rate, a delay in movement or a sim running slowly. *Frame-rate* refers to the frames per second the video is running at within the viewer, therefore the higher the frame-rate the smoother and better the user experience. We can check our current frame-rate (**FPS**) from the **Basic** section of the **Statistics** window ([**Ctrl**] + [**Shift**] + [**1**]).

```
Basic
FPS                              14.6 fps
0.0          15.0        30.0         45.0
Bandwidth                     145 kbps
Packet Loss                     0.0 %
Ping Sim                      206 msec
Advanced
Simulator
```

Lag may occur when:

* There are too many objects and textures in view for your system to easily cope with.

* There are a large number of other avatars nearby.

* You are moving and therefore the Second Life viewer is loading new geometry, textures, and sounds.

* Objects are moving and therefore the Second Life viewer is loading new geometry, textures, and sounds.

* You have too many graphics features enabled for your system to easily cope with (e.g. local lighting, reflections, shadows, etc.).

Server-side lag

If you recall, each region within Second Life runs on a single independent CPU. Server-side lag describes slow-down either within this CPU, often created by the region's environment (e.g. a badly designed sim) or by wider sim/grid/server issues.

Causes of server-side lag

* **Textures:** Every time an avatar enters a region the region's CPU needs to download the textures into their cache. Therefore regions with high numbers of high resolution textures may run more slowly.

* **Scripts:** Every time a script runs it runs on the region's CPU. Too many or badly written scripts may cause the region to run more slowly.

- **Movement:** Every time either an object or texture moves the region's CPU has to re-calculate how the object appears relative to any residents viewing it. Too many moving objects or textures may cause the region to run more slowly.

- **Physics:** For example, when two objects collide the region's CPU must calculate the result of that collision for both objects and relay the information to any nearby avatars. Therefore regions experiencing a high numbers of collisions may run more slowly.

- **Wider grid issues:** Server-side lag can also be caused by any number of impossible-to-specify Second Life grid issues.

As a resident there is not much you can do about server-side lag except report your difficulties if so inclined (not to me please!). To check if you are experiencing server-side lag, select **Help > Lag Meter** from the viewer's top menu to display a lag meter.

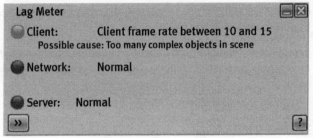

The Lag Meter monitors the client, network and server lag and details the possible causes. My experience (as in this image) is that if you are experiencing lag, and the Second Life grid is functioning normally, it will be client-side lag that will be the issue.

Client-side lag

Client-side lag is produced within a user's own system. Information regarding changes in textures and objects must be transmitted from a region's server to each resident's Second Life viewer (technically referred to as the *client*). If the client cannot either download or process this information rapidly enough then the unfortunate result is an ever increasing queue of unprocessed data; AKA client-side lag.

If you are experiencing high levels of client-side lag you can upgrade parts or all of your system and/or tweak your system and preferences.

Setting up for best performance

Computer systems are different and therefore there is no panacea to solve lag issues. But if you are suffering under-performance issues you can work down the following checklist. Some suggestions involve spending money but most do not.

System

* It is certainly preferable that your system comfortably exceeds the Second Life viewer's minimum system requirements. An older (over 3 years!) CPU or graphics card or low RAM memory can contribute to client-side lag. Consider upgrading these components of your system.

* Regularly defrag your hard drive and clean your Registry (see page 17).

* Regularly clear the cache from the **Edit > Preferences > Network** tab.

Internet connection/network

* Ensure you have a DSL or cable broadband connection. **Any** other type of connection (even if it claims to be broadband) may not produce a usable experience with Second Life.

* Display the Statistics bar ([**Ctrl**] + [**Shift**] + [**1**]) and note your **Ping Sim** and **Packet Loss** values. The Ping Sim value is the time (in milliseconds) data takes to reach the server from your computer. If this number is high (over a few hundred msec.), it could indicate a problem with your Internet connection. If the Packet Loss value is a non-zero number, your network or ISP may be having issues.

If you're getting a significant amount of packet loss you may need to adjust your Maximum Bandwidth on the **Edit > Preferences > Network** tab. Using the slider reduce the Maximum Bandwidth setting until the packet loss stops. If your system is not experiencing packet loss then raise the Maximum Bandwidth setting as far as it will go.

Graphics card

Your system's graphics card is kept frantically busy within the constantly and rapidly changing environment experienced within Second Life.

- Ensure your system has a Second Life compatible graphics card installed. Non-compatible cards may work but are likely to be problematic when displaying the Second Life world.

- Ensure you have the manufacturer's latest graphic card drivers installed.

CPU

The CPU does a lot of work in Second Life compared with most other applications. Unless you have a very powerful system Second Life will almost certainly run your CPU at 100% the entire time you have the viewer running.

- You may need to reduce your Maximum Bandwidth on the **Edit > Preferences > Network** tab if your CPU is receiving more data than it can process.

Memory

- Close all other applications when running the Second Life software.

- Rebooting your system before starting the Second Life viewer can increase available system memory.

Adjusting viewer preferences

- **Edit > Preferences > Network** tab. If you can afford the disk space then set your disk cache size to 1000Mb, otherwise set it as high as you can afford.

- **Edit > Preferences > Graphics** tab. Move the **Quality and Performance Slider** to Low (Faster).

Graphics tab options

Tick the Custom box, then set these options:

- Un-tick all the **Shaders:** checkboxes (i.e. bump mapping, reflections, etc.).

- Reduce the **Draw Distance** to 64m.

- Reduce **Max. Particle Count** to less than 1,000.

- Reduce all the **Mesh Detail sliders** to low (i.e. objects, trees etc.).

- **Avatar Rendering:** Tick Avatar Imposters.

- **Terrain Detail:** Select Low.

- **Lighting Detail:** Select Sun and moon only.

Irie tip

Never tick the 'Atmospheric Shaders' checkbox unless you specifically require these effects either when taking images or during warm romantic evenings in quiet locations. Drawing clouds racing across the sky requires a considerable amount of your system's resources!

Click **Hardware Options:**

- **Filtering:** uncheck.

- **Texture Memory:** set to Large.

Managing these settings correctly ensures that less information is received by your system and therefore less data needs to be processed. Once you have eliminated the primary sources of lag then you can review and re-enable any options that don't cause your system to suffer too much.

Freezing

On occasions your avatar may perform or move unusually in a manner such as marching off into the distance or freezing still. This most commonly occurs when an avatar is crossing region boundaries but can happen anywhere. Take your fingers off the movement arrows and wait for a few moments. If the situation does not improve then you will need to restart the Second Life application (perhaps using the opportunity to clear the cache and reboot your system).

At any given moment your viewer is connected to several different Second Life servers (such as the region server, the inventory asset databases, cash balance servers, etc.). If your avatar cannot walk or can only rotate on the spot then this indicates that the viewer has become disconnected from one or more of these servers; a mini-crash if you like. If this happens then you will need to restart the Second Life application.

Irie tip

A quick teleport can sometimes save the day! [Shift] + [Ctrl] + [H] will TP you to your home location and sometimes will solve a freezing issue.

If the Ping Sim value (from the Statistics window [Ctrl] + [Shift] + [1]) is 10,000 msec. then you have 'silently' crashed and will need to restart the Second Life viewer.

Objects and items

Within Second Life an *object* describes any prim or collection of linked prims. An object may be as simple as a one-prim box or as complex as the 156 prim lion sculpture opposite.

An *item* may be an object, but the item class also includes non-objects such as textures, animations and articles of Second Life clothing (i.e. shirt, jacket, etc.).

To keep track with the millions of items rendered in-world and hoarded within residents' inventories, each item is assigned a unique code (universal unique identifier or UUID). For example, the

lion's UUID is 9e9c383f-8671-9e7f-7e7d-f52af24f54f3. This UUID is commonly referred to as the *key*. An item's details (i.e. item name, creator, owner, shape, colour, position, etc.) are stored alongside the key on Second Life servers. The systems that manage items are technically referred to as *Asset Servers* and *Asset Databases*.

Irie note

The lion's UUID is taken from a single parent or root prim within the collection of linked prims. The keys, details and relevant positions of all the other 155 prims attached to it are stored alongside the key of this parent prim.

Item permissions

Item permissions are applied to limit what residents may do with the items they possess.

An item's permissions are viewed and set either:

In-world:

1 Right-click the object then select **Edit** from the pie menu (ensure that the full menu is played: click the **More>>** button if necessary).

2   Locate the **You can:** section of the **Edit** menu.

Or

From Inventory:

1   Open the Inventory (**[Ctrl] + [I]**) and locate the item.

2   Right-click on the item and select **Properties** from the drop-down menu.

3   Locate the **You can:** section of the **Inventory Item Properties** window.

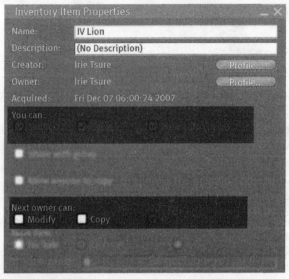

Inventory Item Properties windows

Contained within the **You can:** section are the three permissions checkboxes of which at least one must be ticked.

Copy permission

When ticked, the **Copy** permission, unsurprisingly, permits the item's owner to copy the item, i.e.:

• When a copy-able (copy) item is rendered in-world or trans-ferred to another resident (subject to transfer permissions) then it is the copy of the item that is rendered or transferred. The original item always remains within the inventory.

- When a no-copy object is rendered in-world then the object will leave the inventory until taken back from the grid and returned to the inventory.

- A no-copy item is removed from your inventory when it is transferred to another resident (subject to transfer permissions).

Modify permission

When ticked, the Modify permission permits us to edit an item. Modifying allows residents, for example, to re-size clothing items or change the texture of an object.

Resell/Give Away permission (Transfer)

The Resell/Give Away permission is commonly referred to as *Transfer*. When ticked, the transfer permission permits residents to give the item to another resident.

Irie note

A copy object cannot contain a no-copy item and similarly a transferable object cannot contain a no-transfer item.

An item that can be copied, modified and transferred is referred to as *Full Perm*. A resident has full perms on all items they create.

Item owners may remove next owner permissions from items by un-ticking the relevant checkbox from the **Next owner can:** section beneath. Item owners may not grant to the next owner item permissions that they do not already possess themselves.

Interacting with objects

Wherever residents go in-world we find a multitude of objects to interact with.

To interact with objects we simply click on them. With a left-click we first investigate whether the creator intends an object to perform a specific function such as delivering a notecard or selling and delivering a product, otherwise right-clicking an object will access the object's pie menu. Within this pie-menu, and from the list below, the object's available functions will be highlighted:

Pay

A payment dialog box is displayed when the **Pay** segment is available and selected.

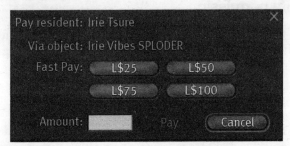

The pay dialog box offers a **Fast Pay** option (either a single figure or choice of figures) and/or an empty **Amount** box for you to enter your own figure. When you select the **Pay** (or any **Fast Pay** button) then this amount is taken from your L$ account and paid to the owner of the object. You will come across the pay function most commonly when using vendor objects and tip-jar objects. Tip jars are used by residents to send gratuities to deserving performers and venues.

Take

When the **Take** segment is available then you have the necessary permissions to take the object from the Second Life grid and into your inventory. This most likely means that you are the owner of the object. When you select **Take**, the object will disappear from the Second Life grid and be transferred into your inventory.

Sit Here

When the **Sit Here** segment is available, you can attempt to sit your avatar on the object whether it was designed to be sat upon or not. If there is no suitable surface on which to sit your avatar, then an on-screen message will be displayed to this effect. The creator of the object does have the facility to change the descriptive text of the **Sit Here** segment of the pie-menu and as such you may find other descriptive words displayed in it such as 'Sit', 'Dance', 'Ride', 'Sleep', etc. The **Sit Here** function is commonly applied to chairs, all manner of pose-balls, vehicles, etc.

Touch

When the **Touch** segment is available, you can click the object to see if any subsequent function is triggered. This subsequent function may, for example, be the delivery of a landmark or notecard, may direct you to a web page or open another dialog box offering any number of further options. The creator of the object does have the facility to change the text of the **Touch** segment of the pie menu and as such you may find other descriptive words displayed in it.

Create

When the **Create** segment is available, you have the necessary parcel permissions to build and when selected, the **Creation** menu will be displayed. This segment seems to have little to do with the object we click on, but is a quick and easy way to access the **Creation** menu. The pointer (cursor) transforms into a wand and wherever you then click, a new prim will be rendered (see Chapter 8).

Open

Objects can and often do contain other items within them (other objects, landmarks, notecards, etc.). When the **Open** segment is available then this indicates that the selected object does contain at least one other item. Selecting **Open** will access the **Object Contents** window listing the items contained within.

When the **Copy To Inventory** button is available, it indicates that you have the necessary permissions to copy (or transfer) these contents to your inventory. The **Copy And Wear** button will only be available when the object contains items that can be 'worn' (i.e. prim objects and Second Life clothing items). The Open function is most commonly applied to single prim boxes in order to facilitate the simple delivery of purchased products.

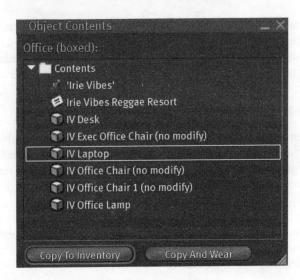

Edit...

When the **Edit** segment is available then you have the necessary permissions to edit the object and when selected, the **Edit** menu will be displayed.

More >

Selecting **More >** from this pie menu accesses further functions again displayed in the form of a pie menu.

Return...

If the **Return** segment is available then you have the necessary permissions to return this object from the Second Life grid and into the object owner's *Inventory > Lost And Found* folder. If you are the owner of the object it will be returned to your own *Lost And Found* folder. Once you select **Return** the object will disappear from the Second Life grid.

Attach >

Objects can be attached to avatars. Selecting **Attach >** accesses another pie menu system listing all the parts of an avatar's body to which objects may be attached. If you have the necessary permissions to attach an object then selecting a body part from the pie menu will attach this object to the selected attachment point. And yes, if you have the necessary permissions then you can attach anything to anywhere. We most commonly witness this as a mistake in the form of confused newbies with boxes attached to their heads as they try to 'wear' the boxed hairpiece they have just acquired (we've all done it) but such a mistake can also and easily manifest even more embarrassing and un-fashionable accessories such as trees, buildings, speedboats, etc.

Attach HUD >

The HUD (Head Up Display) allows residents to display objects within their main Second Life viewer window. HUDs are not visible to other residents. HUDs can be gadgets such as avatar radars, personal building aids, personal dance/animation players (commonly known in-world as a Chimera or **Chim**), sound generators etc. and are used to simplify residents' in-world experiences. Selecting **Attach HUD >** will display another pie menu listing all the areas of the Second Life viewer to which objects may be attached. If you have the necessary permissions to attach an object then selecting a HUD area from the pie menu will attach the selected object to the selected HUD point.

Take Copy

When the **Take Copy** segment is available then you have the necessary permissions to take a copy of the object. When you select **Take Copy** a copy of the object will be placed in your inventory but the original object will remain in situ on the Second Life grid.

Wear

Objects may be attached to your avatar. Selecting the **Wear** segment will attach the object to the intended attachment point.

Delete

When the **Delete** segment is available you have the necessary permissions to delete the object from the Second Life grid and into the object owner's *Inventory* > *Lost And Found* folder. If you are the object's owner then the object will be returned to your *Inventory* > *Trash* folder. When you select **Delete** the object will disappear from the Second Life grid.

Buy

If the object is, or its contents are, for sale then the **Buy** segment will be available for selection. The object's owner will have set the price and decided whether buying it will deliver to the purchaser:

- **The original** (including any transferable contents): in this case the object remains in situ in-world but the ownership of it transfers to the purchaser.

- **A copy** (including any copy-able and transferable contents): in this case the object remains in situ in-world and a copy of it is delivered to the inventory of the purchaser.

- **The contents**: in which case the object remains in situ in-world and a copy of its transferable contents are delivered to the inventory of the buyer.

More >

Selecting **More >** from this pie menu displays further functions again in the form of a pie menu.

Report Abuse...

Selecting the **Report Abuse** segment displays a window in which residents can report for investigation, objects that violate the Second Life Terms of Service. Such an object may for example be one encroaching into another resident's parcel or one persistently producing annoying noises or images.

Inspect

Selecting the **Inspect** segment displays a window detailing information about the object including the name, owner, creator and creation date of each individual prim within the object.

Mute

Some objects talk, shout, deliver notecards, landmarks, etc. Selecting the **Mute** segment silences an object for a resident and automatically declines any object or item it attempts to deliver. Muting an object does not affect its interaction with any other resident.

Acquiring some money

It certainly is not essential to have any Linden dollars to participate in Second Life but acquiring a little local currency can be both fun and useful. Your Linden dollar balance is displayed to the left of the search box on the top menu bar of the viewer.

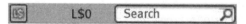

Experienced Second Life business owners are understandably a little reluctant to employ inexperienced or new residents therefore as a newbie and depending on your personal circumstances you have two realistic open avenues to acquire some quick cash.

All residents can buy Linden dollars from a number of online sources. (You will find a link to the International L$ Marketplace from the LindeX™ Exchange web page of the main Second Life website.) Second Life Premium account holders can buy their dollars from the Linden Dollar Exchange 'LindeX™' by clicking the L$ button next to the Linden Dollar Balance. The common alternative to buying dollars is to raise funds by camping.

Camping

A parcel's or venue's popularity can be measured in *traffic*. A parcel's traffic figure is the result of a calculation reflecting how many residents visited a particular parcel and for how long they stayed. The higher the traffic figure then the higher up the Places search results the parcel will be found. Campers are residents paid by businesses to stay on the same parcel in order to raise this traffic figure. A few hours' camping gives many new residents enough Linden dollars to enable them to buy their first items.

To find a camping station type 'camp', 'camping', 'free lindens', 'free money' or similar search-term into the search box then teleport to a parcel that sponsors camping.

Camping systems may be static in nature, for example a chair or bench can be designed to pay any resident that sits down, but more and more camping systems are becoming board-based. Board-based camping systems permit residents to commence camping by touching the board and then campers can continue to be paid as they move around the parcel.

Irie tip

If while camping, your avatar becomes logged off then your camping session will be discontinued. If you want to camp while you are away from your keyboard (AFK) then don't forget to uncheck **Advanced > Character > Character Tests > Go Away/AFK When Idle** from the top menu bar (**[Ctrl] + [Alt] + [D]** to toggle the **Advanced Menu**).

The pay rate for camping will be displayed in the floating text above the camping object or on a signboard close by. Camping rates usually vary up to about L$10 per hour. Once you have chosen your preferred camping station then either sit on the camping object or to activate a board-based camping system, touch the board then follow the instructions.

Shopping

Once you have acquired some Linden dollars you may want to do some shopping. If you are looking for specific items such as hair, clothes, etc. then make good use of the Second Life search window. Explore and sharpen results by using the **Classified** and **Places** tabs on the Search window and also by using keyword searching, Boolean logic and phrase searching (see page 57).

Your purchased items may be delivered to your inventory either contained within a single boxed object or placed within a new folder. The most straightforward route to locating recent purchases is to select the **Recent Items** tab of the **Inventory** window.

To access boxed object purchases:

1 Find a parcel such as a public sandbox in which you can render the box in-world.

2 Render the box object by dragging it from your inventory and onto the ground.

3 Open the box (**right-click > Open**) then copy the object's contents to your inventory.

4 Don't forget to be tidy and **Take** or **Delete** the empty box once you have copied or transferred its contents to your inventory.

I built my in-world businesses from freebies and this, combined with the fact that I've dressed in pretty much the same style of basic casual clothing since my arrival, means that though I may be considered an expert in many departments, shopping is not one of them (though I do occasionally dress up for formal events and even purchased a suit for the cover image!). However my friends list does boast some of the most stylish shopaholic fashionistas ever to grace the Second Life grid. I spoke with the eternally elegant and stylish shopping 'queen of queens' Eve Parnall in order to glean some insight. Though Eve's tips are fashion orientated many of her words of advice apply equally when shopping for any other type of products.

Eve Parnall's Second Life shopping tips

+ Do not close the search window as you teleport between store locations. Leave the window open or minimize it so you will not need to redefine your search.

+ For more choice visit the retailer's main-store. You will usually find the landmark in all the retailer's smaller outlets.

+ Examine the store's traffic figure from the About Land window to see how popular they are with other residents (top menu **World > About Land...**).

- Look for a free version. Free stores often have adequate products including skin, hair, clothes and shoes.

- When available, try out a demo version before purchasing a product to ensure it looks good on your avatar.

- Check the item permissions if you think that you may wish to resize, re-colour or transfer your purchase.

- Look for ways to obtain a discount card from your favourite stores.

- Take a landmark of your preferred retail outlets so that you can easily return to them (top menu **World > Create Landmark Here**).

- To receive discounts and notices of new products join the groups of the creators and retailers that you are most impressed with.

- If you see another resident who looks particularly cool or stylish then open their profile and examine their groups and their Picks. Stylish residents often belong to their favourite retailers' groups in order to receive discounts and notices of new products.

- Ask fashionable residents for a landmark for the store in which they bought their outfits. Most residents will be delighted to help you and this is a fun way to make new and trendy friends.

- In the event of an issue such as a failed delivery you may be asked to provide details of the transaction. Each one (including L$0 ones) is uniquely numbered. Details of all your transactions during the last 30 days are accessed by clicking the Transactions History link on the My Account page. More extensive lists can also be downloaded as XML files from this web page.

Managing your inventory

Our inventories rapidly fill up with thousands and potentially tens of thousands of items. To find out how many items you currently have stored in your inventory, type any letter into the Search field at the top of the Inventory window, wait a few moments then the item count will display in the title bar.

Much advice implores Second Life residents to organize their inventories for example and I quote *'before things get completely out of hand and confusing'*. Oh please! The reality is that with

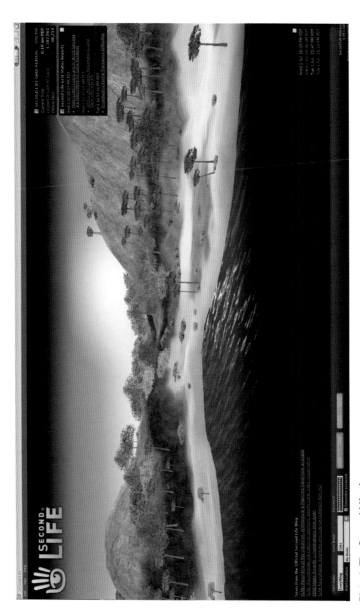

Plate 1: The Second Life viewer

Plate 2: Arriving in Second Life

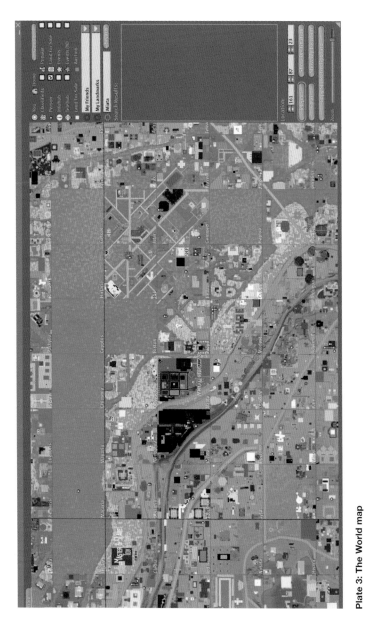

Plate 3: The World map

Plate 4: Functional art

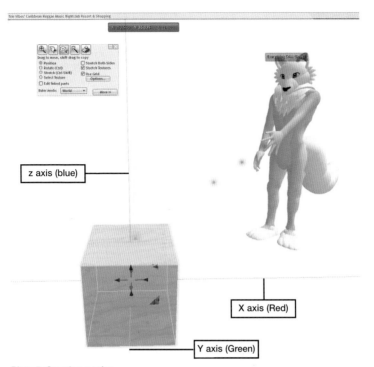

z axis (blue)

X axis (Red)

Y axis (Green)

Plate 5: Creating a prim

Plate 6: Sculpted fruit by Qarl Linden

Plate 7: Using the lighting features

```
key gOwner;
default
{
    state_entry()
    {
        llSay(0, "Hello, Avatar!");
    }

    touch_start(integer num_detected)
    {
    gOwner = llGetOwner();
        if (llDetectedKey(0) == gOwner)
        {
            llSay(0, "Hello Boss!");
            llSay(0, "Sending you to the kitchen");
            state kitchen;
        }
        else
            llSay(0, "Hello Avatar!");
    }
}

state kitchen
{
    state_entry()
    {
        llSay(0, "Welcome to the kitchen Avatar!");
    }

    touch_start(integer num_detected)
    {
        gOwner = llGetOwner();
        if (llDetectedKey(0) == gOwner)
        {
            llSay(0, "Hello Boss!");
            llSay(0, "Sending you to the hallway.");
            state default;
        }
        else
        {
            llSay(0, "Are you lost?");
            state default;
        }
    }
}
```

Plate 8: Colour makes scripts easier to follow

Plate 9: Find an outlet for your creativity in Second Life

no limit to the number of items that residents can store within their inventory and a simple filter and incorporated search system, organizing our inventories seems (to me anyway) both a fairly lowly priority and hideously time-consuming. The bottom line is that you should name your objects appropriately then use the search field to locate them within your inventory and not waste time scrolling.

But just in case you feel the urge to be neat here's how I would go about managing my inventory (in the extremely unlikely event that I ever get the urge to tidy up).

Residents can create as many folders and subfolders as we want by selecting **Create > New Folder** from the **Inventory** window menu bar or by right-clicking an existing folder then selecting **New Folder** from the drop-down menu. We may then rename these folders with a right-click on the new folder then selecting **Rename** from the drop-down menu. This facilitates dividing our inventory into manageable and logical sections and therefore items may be located easily.

My current inventory management basically extends as far as creating one new folder named *Purse* in which I keep my hair, coffee, shotgun and the other items I feel I may need to locate in a hurry. I have a star at the beginning of this folder name to ensure that it appears first when the inventory folders are listed alphabetically (select **Sort > Folders Always By Name** from the Inventory window menu bar).

Irie note

Icon-displaying system folders such as Animations, Body Parts, Objects, etc. cannot be moved, renamed or deleted.

We can choose to sort our inventory either alphabetically by item name or chronologically by the date the item was acquired.

To sort inventory items alphabetically:

1 Open the iinventory ([Ctrl] + [I]).

2 Select **Sort > By Name** from the Inventory window menu bar.

To sort inventory items chronologically:

1   Open the inventory.

2   Select **Sort > By Date** from the Inventory window menu-bar.

Some useful inventory features

Drag and drop

Folders and items can be dragged between one inventory location and another. Click, hold then drag any folder or item (with [Ctrl] to select multiple folders or items). Release the button once the cursor is over the destination folder.

Multi-view

We can display two or more inventory windows at the same time by selecting **File > New Window** from the Inventory window menu bar. We can then more easily drag subfolders and items to new folder locations by maintaining a different view in each inventory.

Irie parable

The one time I desperately needed a high-prim drum kit was unfortunately within a few days of deleting the highly detailed freebie ('I'll never ever ever use that') 'band in a box'. At that moment I vowed never to delete another item from my inventory however abstract and unusable it seemed.

Listening to music and viewing media in-world

Residents may choose to stream music and/or play media (currently an image, a video or a web page) across their own land parcels or across parcels on which they have the necessary Group abilities (see Groups, page 97).

* To hear a parcel's available music stream select the **Audio &** **Video** tab from the **Preferences** window ([Ctrl] + [P]) then tick the **Play Streaming Music When Available** checkbox.

Irie note

Your computer system must be connected (usually via a soundcard device) to a functioning speaker system in order to be able to listen to streaming music.

---

* To view a parcel's available media select the **Play Streaming Media When Available** option on the same tab.

After selecting these options and when you subsequently visit a land parcel that is streaming music and/or media then your viewer's music and/or media play buttons will become active (lighten).

Music   Media   Volume

Click the appropriate play button to listen to the stream or view the media.

Photography and video

The Second Life viewer has a Snapshot function used to record images of residents' in-world views. We have the choice whether to save these pictures to our system's hard drive, email them as a postcard or upload them to our Second Life inventory. Uploading a Snapshot to Inventory is charged at L$10 per image.

To take a snapshot:

1   Frame the viewer to include the image you wish to capture.

2   Click on the **Snapshot** button or use the keyboard shortcut [Ctrl] + [Shift] + [S] to capture the image.

   The **Snapshot Preview** window is displayed which includes a thumbnail preview of your snapshot.

3   From the **What would you like to do?** section of the Snapshot Preview window, select one of the following radio buttons:

* **Send a postcard** to email the image. (When you click the **Send** button a Postcard window will be displayed which includes a recipient's email address field, a subject field and a message box.)

* **Upload a snapshot** to save the image to your inventory. Your in-world account will be charged L$10 as the file will be stored on Second Life servers.

* **Save snapshot to hard drive** to save the image to your hard drive.

4 Tick the **Show interface in snapshot** checkbox if you want the user interface (i.e. toolbars, windows, menus, etc.) to be captured in your snapshot.

5 Tick the **Show HUD objects in snapshot checkbox** if you want any attached HUD(s) to be captured in the snapshot.

6 We need to click the **Refresh Snapshot** button in order to capture in the snapshot, any changes to these two settings.

Irie tip

To save money, I always save snapshots to my hard drive and only pay to upload those pictures I wish to use in-world.

7   Depending on the selection within the **What would you like to do?** section of the Snapshot Preview window, click either the **Send, Upload,** or **Save** button to complete the process.

Irie tip

We can quickly save one or more screenshots to our system's hard drive using the shortcut **[Ctrl] + [']**.

Recording video

The Second Life viewer also offers a simple and built-in video capture function to record video of what we see in-world. Video is saved to our system's hard-drive and can consume a considerable amount of hard drive space.

Irie tip

When we are recording video we can hide the Second Life user interface (UI) using the shortcut **[Ctrl] + [Alt] + [1]**.

To start recording video:

1   Select **File > Start/Stop Movie to Disk** (or use the shortcut **[Ctrl] + [Shift] + [A]**) to open the Save dialog box and select the location (for ease of access I usually save to the Desktop).

2   Select a compression option from the **Video Compression** dialog box. If you are not sure which to choose then select **Full Frames (Uncompressed).**

3   Click **OK.**

To stop recording video:

♦   Select **File > Start/Stop Movie to Disk** (or use the shortcut **[Ctrl] + [Shift] + [A]**).

Irie note

We can edit the video files we capture with free programs such as Windows Movie Maker or iMovie for the Mac.

06

socializing in second life

In this chapter you will learn:

- about your profile
- where and how to meet other residents
- how to find events and join groups
- how to use and make gestures
- about the Voice feature

Filling in your profile

We start to convey a little about ourselves by filling in the various editable sections of our Second Life Profile. We display our profile either by clicking directly on our avatar then selecting **Profile...** from the pie menu or alternatively by selecting **Edit > Profile...** from the viewer's top menu bar.

From the **2nd Life** tab of the profile, residents can display any texture/photo contained within their inventory (left-click on the image panel to change the texture) and also to describe ourselves and/or articulate our values by typing text in the **About:** section.

The **Web, Interests** and **Picks** tabs all offer opportunities for us to share with other residents further information about ourselves, our skills, ambitions and favourite Second Life destinations.

Irie tip

I suggest you do not complete the **1st Life** tab of your profile until you are certain whether or not you wish to divulge your real-world identity. Perhaps it would be wise to settle in before you decide what you want to do with your **1st Life** tab.

Meeting other residents

It is the social networking element of Second Life that is the primary draw for most residents and originally was the stated purpose of the Second Life project. Whether it is romance or meeting new friends that we have in mind or relating to like-minded (e.g. creative) residents, discovering new interests, interacting with far-flung real-world friends and relatives or even creating a new community, the possibilities for social interaction are as unlimited within Second Life as are the creative possibilities of the environment.

Second Life is also a gloriously multinational and wonderfully multicultural society populated by residents representing scores of nations, languages and cultures. Some regions are nationally or culturally themed, for example, I hope our region of Irie succeeds in reflecting some of the positive cultural identity of the

West Indies. The Second Life grid therefore provides a unique opportunity for us to socialize incredibly easily and in real time within an amazingly diverse and rich community.

Irie sermon

Let me take this opportunity to explode a patently ridiculous myth. It is often convenient for residents to verbalize and accept the notion that because we interact within Second Life using remotely controlled avatars our feelings and the feelings of other residents are somehow disengaged from the process. The truth of course is that when I am fond of a particular resident then I actually care, when somebody makes me happy in-world then I am genuinely joyful and if any resident insults or tramples over my avatar then I am (to a greater or lesser extent) personally offended and hurt.

Though the social process of Second Life is both remote and as anonymous as an individual wishes, please never forget that behind every avatar in Second Life is an operator; a real-world person dealing with their personal portion of bad days, human frailties and emotional insecurities.

There are no such things as 'virtual feelings'!

As role-players make up a significant proportion of residents, it is both perfectly acceptable to refuse to discuss your own real life and wise to consider that any 'real life' details presented by another resident may be part of their role-playing experience. Beware! The 21-year-old, six-foot Brazilian centrefold before you may, in fact, be a 47-year-old father of two from Manchester.

Many residents choose to express themselves in terms of super-model dimensions. Short, squat or less-than-stunning residents are not the norm. One resident finding another resident attractive is therefore neither surprising nor unusual. The vistas are stunning, the music divine and residents dance closely together using the synchronized animations offered by pose-balls. We can then hold hands while we stroll through magical forests or along tropical beaches. We can sit, watch the sun go down (again and again if we so please) then chat the remainder of night away. We can hug and kiss our new friend. We can choose to move our relationship onto a physical level.

Sex

Reflecting the wider Internet (and perhaps society in general?), sex and 'adult-orientated' regions and businesses of Second Life seem to dominate much of the landscape. The reality is that only offering residents free money appears to compete with the attraction of escorts, strip joints and free sex rooms and most residents will have at least dipped a metaphoric toe during their early explorations of Second Life. Some find the experience banal whilst others are stimulated by virtual sex and it becomes an important feature of their Second Life experience.

On a practical level, residents create and retail highly detailed and physically accurate skins for residents to wear. 'Additional' body parts can be attached to an avatar in the same way as any other object. These attached 'body parts' can be and often are scripted to function and react in imaginative ways. And to complete the scene, animations are available offering a multitude of solo, couple and group positions and 'activities'.

Romance and partnerships

Romantic relationships seem to develop in-world with a frightening 'hyper-speed' encouraged perhaps by the relative anonymity and the apparent lack of consequences within the environment. Second Life couples may register a relationship and have their partner's identity displayed on their Profile. Creating a partnership costs each partner L$10 and some entrepreneurial residents offer venues and the experienced staff to conduct these 'marriages'.

Second Life divorce can be brutal. Separation is managed unilaterally, immediately and costs only L$25. In any world being abandoned by a partner is a hard knock to take and hard knocks do leave dents.

But some romances develop. I know residents who have met in-world only to see their relationship flourish into the real world. A few are currently happily married in real life. Amazing isn't it?!

The Second Life Showcase

The Second Life Showcase is perhaps the surest way to find those in-world venues that command the highest levels of resident interest. The Showcase is accessed either online from a link on the homepage (www.secondlife.com) or in-world from the Search window ([Ctrl] + [F] > **Showcase** tab).

The Showcase is an editorially-controlled directory for which venues are selected to highlight Second Life's finest user-created locations. It suggests in-world locations in the categories of Music, Hot Spots, Arts & Culture, Fashion and Photos & Machinima.

Finding events

There are hundreds of resident hosted in-world events every day. These Events feature attractions such as live performances, discussions, sales, games, exhibitions and workshops.

The Second Life Events calendar can be accessed and displayed either from the Second Life website or in-world from the Search window ([Ctrl] + [F]).

Using the All tab

We search events from the Search window's **All** tab by entering a keyword, selecting **Events** from the category drop-down menu (default **Any Category**) then clicking the **Search** button. The events names and descriptions will be searched for your keyword and relevant results displayed accordingly.

Clicking on an event listed in the Results window displays the name and limited details of the event with a **Teleport** and a **View Full Profile** button.

Clicking the button accesses the **Event Information** window in which fuller details of the event are displayed including **Show on Map**, **Notify** and **Create Event** buttons.

Selecting the **Notify** button will ensure an in-world message is delivered to you prior to the event starting.

To cancel the notification, click on the newly appeared **Don't Notify** button.

Irie note

Searching Events using the **All** tab may display events that have already concluded and the results are not listed in chronological order.

Using the Events tab

Using the Search window **Events** tab is certainly a more controlled method of browsing and identifying Events to attend.

Entering no criteria and clicking the Search button will return in the left panel of the Search window all today's scheduled events starting with those events in progress and upcoming.

Selecting an event from the left panel will display in the right panel the details and description of the event as well as **Teleport**, **Show on Map** and **Notify** buttons.

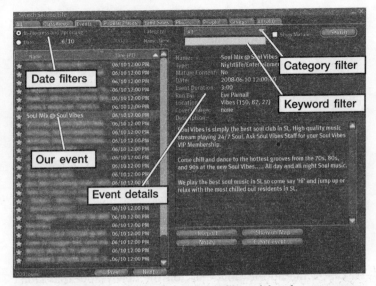

The search results for events can be filtered by date, category and/or keyword.

* **Date:** Selecting the **Date** radio button (by default the **In-Progress and Upcoming** button is selected) activates the date controls, then by clicking the **<<** or **>>** buttons we can display the previous or next day's events respectively. Selecting the **Today** button re-displays current in-world events.

* **Category:** Selecting the **Category** drop-down menu displays the categories that events can be listed under. Selecting a category then clicking the **Search** button will display only those events listed within the selected category.

* **Keyword:** Entering a keyword or search term in the **Name/Desc:** box searches events by keyword. This search is seriously limited in that only those events are displayed in which the inputted keyword is identical to the *first* word of the event name. The keyword filter is therefore only really useful in searching for events that you are certain of the event name and far less useful for a general browse.

Second Life groups

Second Life groups are in-world collectives that residents form, join and belong to. Groups may be business or venue-related, organizations, social societies or just a band of friends or like-minded residents. Group members are assigned to specific roles within the group and each role issued with a defining (or amusing) group title. We can discover the groups a resident belongs to from the 2nd Life tab of each resident's profile.

Group titles can be seen above a resident's name in their tag.

This illustrates three group titles defining three distinct roles within a single group. Members that have been assigned different roles within the group will usually possess different group abilities.

By using Second Life groups, residents can also collectively own land. The group members can then be given exclusive access and/or be granted such privileges on the group-owned land as the ability to create objects.

Search for a group

Residents may search for Second Life groups to join by entering a keyword in either the **All** tab or the **Groups** tab of the Second Life Search window ([**Ctrl**] + [**F**]). Once the search results are displayed, click on any group of interest and further details will be displayed.

Joining a group

The way in which residents join a Second Life group depends on whether the group offers *open enrollment* [*sic*]. Groups offering this are available for anyone to join simply by clicking the **Join** button (**N.B.** a group may charge a fee to join).

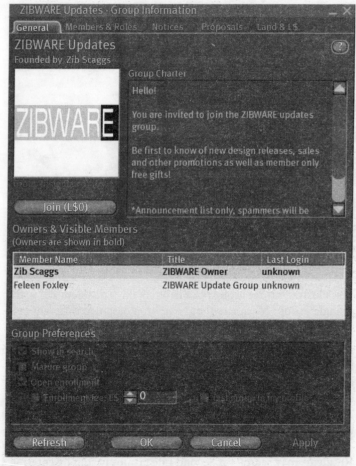

To join a Second Life group that does not offer open enrolment requires a personal invitation from either the group owner or from an existing group member who has been granted the ability to invite other residents to join the group. Second Life residents can belong to a maximum of 25 groups at any one time.

The Active group

Though residents may belong to numerous groups only one group can be *active*.

A resident's active group influences such abilities as whether the resident can enter group-restricted land or whether a scripted object recognizes their avatar as a group member. Most commonly however, we change active groups in order to change the group title displayed above our name.

To select or change the active group:

1 Select **Edit > Groups** from the top menu-bar of the viewer.

2 Click to select the group you wish to make active (or 'none').

3 Click the **Activate** button.

Your active group (or 'none') will always appear in bold text within this window.

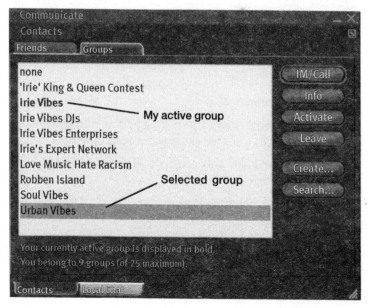

Group liabilities (accounting)

All group members that have assigned to their role the ability to 'Pay group liabilities and receive group dividends' automatically pay an equal share of all group bills. This most commonly occurs when a group-owned parcel is listed within Second Life Search and incurs the L$30 per week charge. This charge is divided between all group members who are assigned the ability to 'Pay group liabilities and receive group dividends'. In turn (but far more unusually) all group members who are assigned this ability automatically receive an equal share of group revenue.

When you have joined a Second Life group make it a habit to check to see whether (without good reason) your role will be required to pay a share of the group's bills.

1 Select **Edit > Groups** from the top menu bar of the viewer.

2 Select the group you wish to check.

3 Click the **Info** button to display the **Group Information** window.

4 From the **Members & Roles** tab select the **Members** tab.

5 Find your avatar's listing by entering part or your entire name into the Search field then clicking the **Search** button.

6 Selecting your name will display both your assigned role(s) and your **Allowed Abilities**.

7 Examine the **Accounting** section of the **Allowed Abilities** section.

In most instances I would immediately leave this group having identified that I will be required to pay group liabilities.

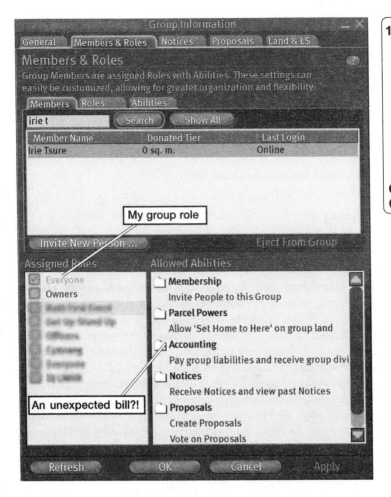

Leaving a group

You can leave any of your Second Life groups at any time. To leave a group:

1 Select **Edit > Groups** from the top menu bar of the Second Life viewer.

2 Select the group you want to leave.

3 Click the **Leave** button.

Second Life etiquette

I get things wrong. Of course I annoy people (ask anyone!). When I upset another resident it is usually unintentional but occasionally it is by being a little too sharp, by forgetting my manners or by allowing myself to become irritated. I try though. I catch and chastise myself when I notice my arrogance rising or my tolerance slipping. That's what I can do.

The following observations serve equally as a reminder to me as they serve as an introduction for you:

* If another resident insults or abuses our avatar then we are likely to become justifiably offended. It is therefore crucial that we appreciate that a real person with real feelings is coupled to every other avatar we meet. Insulting, disrespecting or abusing another resident is never okay.

* Never abuse, attack, embarrass or threaten anyone else no matter what they might have said or done to you. We do come across residents of Second Life who are, for whatever personal reasons, unable to manage their anger or hostility. Other residents seem to have no comprehension of politeness or manners and some even get a kick out of deliberately disturbing the peace of a parcel. Don't become one of these unfortunates; don't permit their issues and weaknesses to reveal your own. The best way to deal with more difficult residents is simply to mute their avatar then report their behaviour to venue staff or to Second Life support if you deem necessary.

Irie note

We mute a resident by right-clicking on either their avatar or title then selecting **Mute** from the pie menu.

* Do not use obscene, offensive or sexually explicit language unless you are certain you are on a parcel where such behaviour is deemed appropriate.

* When you meet another avatar for the first time it is generally considered intrusive and impolite to instant message (IM) them before speaking to them in open chat.

- Typing messages using all capital letters is often considered to be shouting. It should be noted however that a resident using ALL CAPS may be visually impaired or a newbie.

- Never berate or ridicule newbies. We were all newbies not so long ago.

- Do not compose long paragraphs as your conversation partner may get frustrated waiting for your next text to appear. Your chat will be easier to read and digest if you compose a few words, press [Enter] then continue. For example:

  'Hi :-)

  My name is Irie Tsure

  How are you?'

  …is more comfortable to deal with than waiting for:

  'Hi :-), my name is Irie Tsure. How are you?'

- Second Life is not a language test! (unless of course you are using the platform to study a language). Assuming that you are not in an educational environment, when you or another resident makes a typo, if the meaning of what is broadcast is still reasonably clear then there really is no need to make any corrections and absolutely no reason to point out errors in someone else's otherwise clear statement. Just as in the real world (and all too often forgotten), when we communicate it should be what a person is trying to say that is held most important and not their choice of words or the order in which those words are spoken. It is good to remember that many residents make huge efforts to grapple with other tongues than their own and for this we should be grateful. However, if due to a typo the meaning becomes unclear, then text preceded by a star indicates a correction to the previous text. For example:

  'Hi, how is your dork?'

  '*work'

- When we are entering an area it is a good idea to send out a general greeting, e.g. 'Hi everyone!'

- When we notice another resident enter the area, we can make it a point to recognize their presence and welcome them with a friendly: 'Hi (avatar name) :-)'

- When you are ready to leave the parcel it will be appreciated if you bid a general farewell to the group. 'Gotta go to sleep, nite everyone!' is a perfect example.

- It is rude to dominate the conversation by flooding the chat with your own text. Permit other residents to make their fair share of contributions.

- If you do not like the parcel, don't bother moaning, simply go somewhere else.

- Resist openly complaining about parcel lag. Busier parcels inevitably generate a lot more load and anyway it is probably your system that is largely the problem.

- Try extremely hard not to giggle when you see another resident falling from the sky, wearing a box on their head or marching off uncontrollably into the distance and especially when their prim hair or shoes become mis-attached to, shall we say, an unfortunate attachment point!

Some common chat abbreviations

AFK	Away From Keyboard
AV	Avatar
BF	Boy Friend
BRB	Be Right Back
BTW	By The Way
CYA	See you
FYI	For Your Information
GF	Girl Friend
HB	Hurry Back
IMHO	In My Humble Opinion
K or KK	Okay
LOL	Laugh Out Loud
LMAO	Laughing My Ass Off
PLS	Please
RL	Real Life
ROFL	Rolling On Floor Laughing

TTYL	Talk To You Later
TY	Thank You
WB	Welcome Back
WTF	A more earthy variation of 'what the heck!

Irie tip

Using the '/me' command will insert your avatar name in chat. E.g. if I type: '/me is getting tired.', then the broadcast chat will display: 'Irie Tsure is getting tired.'

Gestures

A gesture is a Second Life item that allows residents to trigger animations, sounds and chat text in combination and in a predetermined order. Residents use their gestures to express themselves and to automate certain regularly required responses. We find all our gestures in the *Inventory/Gestures* folder. Right-click any gesture then select **Open** and you will see a **Gesture** window.

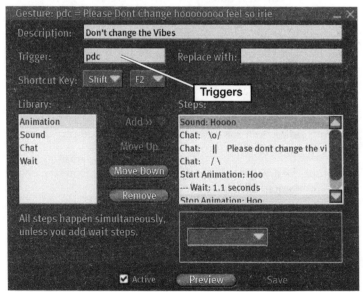

An entertaining example of a gesture, created by my friend Alf.

A gesture will only trigger in-world if the **Active** checkbox is ticked.

Residents often trigger gestures either with a pre-defined function key (e.g. **[Shift]** + **[F2]**) or by typing a specific 'trigger' word or phrase in chat. This gesture has been instructed to trigger in-world whenever I type 'pdc' in chat.

Irie tip

A gesture's **Replace with:** field is used to replace the text in the **Trigger** field. This can be used to save both time and typing. For example if we input 'wb' in the **Trigger** field and 'Welcome back' in the **Replace with** field, once the gesture is active when we subsequently type 'wb' in our chat bar, then 'Welcome back' will be broadcast in open chat. Cool!

We can collectively view all our active gestures in the **Active Gestures** window which is displayed either by selecting **Edit > Gestures** from the Second Life top toolbar or by using the keyboard shortcut **[Ctrl]** + **[G]**. From the Active Gestures window we can play, edit and quickly identify where each gesture is located in our inventory.

Active gestures are also accessible from the **Gestures** drop-down menu to the right of the chat bar. Selecting a gesture from this menu will trigger the gesture in-world.

Creating a new gesture

It is both simple and fun to create and edit new gestures.

1 To create the new gesture item, right-click the *Gestures* folder within the inventory and select **New Gesture** from the drop-down menu.

Or

♦ Select **Create > New Gesture** from the **Inventory** menu bar.

Or

♦ Click the **New** button in the **Active Gestures** window (**[Ctrl]** + **[G]**).

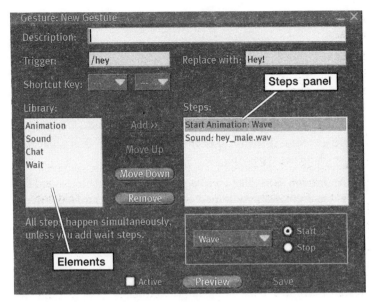

2 Enter a text trigger in the **Trigger** field and/or choose a **Shortcut Key** combination with which to trigger the gesture.

3 Already contained in the **Steps:** panel of a new gesture are two default steps. We want to start from new so to clear the panel, select each step in turn then click the **Remove** button.

4 From the **Library** section of the **Gesture** window select **Animation** then click the **Add>>** button.

5 To enter our first step we select both the **Start** radio button and our first animation element from the displayed drop-down menu.

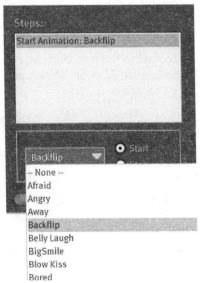

Irie note

An active gesture must have a unique trigger and/or shortcut key. If you activate one that possesses an identical trigger or shortcut key to another active gesture then the originally active one will be deactivated. A pop-up will be displayed to this effect.

There are four element types that can be included in a gesture. These elements types are:

♦ **Animation element:** Your new gesture can include any full perm animation contained within your inventory or inventory library. A looped animation is stopped by inserting, after an appropriate delay (see 'Wait element' below), a **Stop Animation** step.

♦ **Sound element:** Your new gesture can include any full perm sound contained within your inventory or library.

Irie note

All full perm animation and sound items in your inventory will be displayed in the drop-down menu accessible when an animation or sound element is either added to or selected in the Steps: panel.

♦ **Chat element:** Chat to broadcast as part of the gesture is prescribed in the text field displayed when Chat is either added to or selected in the **Steps:** panel. Each Chat step may include up to 127 characters.

♦ **Wait element:** Unless we add Wait steps, all the steps will happen simultaneously. Therefore we insert a Wait step to break the progress of a gesture until, for example, an animation is complete or for a set time while a sound is played. A Wait step may pause a gesture for up to an hour.

6   We now add further animations, wait, chat and sound steps as our creativity takes us. Each element step can be repositioned up or down the Step list using the Move Up and Move Down buttons.

There is a limit to how much information can be contained in a gesture and if that limit is exceeded then an error message will be displayed when we try to save the gesture.

Irie tip

I frequently use the Gesture window **Preview** button to keep my eye on how the new gesture is developing.

---

7   Once we are finished entering gesture steps we should enter a description of our new gesture in the **Description** field.

8   Tick the **Active** checkbox.

9   Click **Save** and close the window.

10 Locate your new gesture using the inventory **Recent Items** tab.

11 Right-click the new gesture, select **Rename** from the drop-down menu then rename it to something memorable.

Using the Voice feature

The Second Life's 3D Voice communication functionality allows residents the option of speaking to one another in real-time. Personally I do not (as yet) use the voice feature to communicate. We discussed in the introduction that Irie Tsure only exists in Second Life and (speaking briefly as Ms Tsure's operator) although Irie shares my real world knowledge and drive, she possesses several additional qualities that I have little chance of ever developing in my own world. For one, Irie Tsure has the wisdom (or opportunity) to briefly consider and revise her words before responding to other residents. Typing responses provides me with the necessary delay (before sending) to edit and therefore limit the damage I would naturally cause with my first (and often worst) reaction. But that's just me. Like every other aspect of

Second Life you will do as you please, so if you would like to explore the Second Life voice feature, here is how:

To use Voice, in addition to a system that at least meets the viewer's minimum requirements, you will need connected to your computer system, either a voice over IP (VoIP) headset or a microphone and speakers. A VoIP headset with a noise-cancelling microphone provides superior sound quality and is preferred.

Irie note

Ensure the land that you are standing on is voice-enabled. An 🔘 icon appears in the viewer's top menu bar if the parcel is voice-enabled. We cannot use the voice feature within parcels that are not voice-enabled.

We turn the voice feature on and off toggling the **Enable Voice** checkbox on the **Voice Chat** tab of the **Preferences** window ([Ctrl] + [P]). Once voice is enabled a white dot (the **Voice Intensity Indicator**) appears above our avatar's head. All voice-enabled residents display a voice intensity indicator and when a resident is speaking normally this emanates pulsing green waves. If these waves turn red, then this indicates that the resident either is speaking too loudly or has their output volume set too high and the resultant speech is likely to be distorted.

My voice intensity indicator

Once voice is enabled, the voice controller is also displayed in the bottom right-hand corner of the Second Life viewer just above the menu bar.

Active speakers

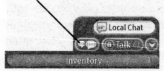

To find nearby voice-enabled residents we display the **Active Speakers** window. We open this from the voice controller with a click on the **Active Speakers** icon to left of the **Talk** button.

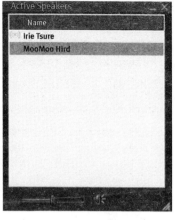

The resident who spoke most recently appears at the top of the Active Speakers list.

We can control the volume of (or mute) another resident by selecting their name from the list then adjusting the volume slider (or clicking the mute button) at the bottom of the window.

We can also use the voice feature to speak exclusively with another resident, a selection of residents or to an entire group irrespective of our in-world locations. Only a single voice session can run at any one time therefore conducting a session with another resident or group means that we cannot hear the residents around us (or participate in any other voice session).

Using Voice to speak with friends

1 Select the **Friends** tab from the **Contacts** tab of the **Communicate** window ([Ctrl] + [T]).

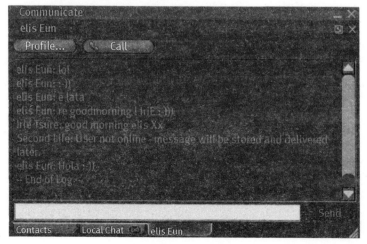

2   Select the name of a voice-enabled friend then click the **IM/ Call** button. The selected friend's IM tab will open.

3   Click the **Call** button at the top of their tab (which will then be replaced with an **End Call** Button).

4   Chat with your friend to your heart's content.

5   Click **End Call** when the conversation is concluded.

Residents may select a number of friends from their Friend's List to invite to a voice session by holding down [**Ctrl**] then clicking in turn on each friend's name. We click the **IM/Call** button once we have selected everyone that we want to invite to join the session.

Using Voice to speak with a Second Life group

Residents can select one of their Second Life groups to conduct a voice session with by selecting the **Groups** tab of the Communicate window then clicking the **IM/Call** button then by following the previous instructions (steps 3–5).

07 owning virtual land

In this chapter you will learn:

- about land and how to find land for sale

- how to buy and sell land

- how to split, join and manage your land parcels

About virtual land

Second Life residents acquire virtual land parcels on which they erect their homes and run their businesses. Second Life land is as defined as either **Mainland** or **Private Estate** (aka Private Islands) and rated as either **PG** or **Mature**.

The PG and Mature ratings of regions reflect the standards commonly applied to the movie industry to denote the age-appropriateness of a given region of Second Life and do not imply that children (U18) are welcome in certain regions of Second Life (older kids can use the Teen Second Life grid). The PG regions intend to offer adult residents an experience free of content such as sexually explicit or violent language, behaviour and imagery.

The **Mainland** is made up of the continents in the middle of the World Map. Mainland is designed, rated and leased to residents by Linden Lab and all Mainland tier payments (monthly maintenance and usage fees) are paid directly to Linden Lab.

Irie note

To own Mainland, a resident must register for a Premium Second Life account using the **Upgrade/Downgrade Account** page accessible from the **My Account** page of the Second Life website.

Residents may own as much Mainland as they choose and then use this land without restrictions other than the region rating and Second Life's TOS. When we change the amount of Mainland we own then the monthly tier payment to Linden Lab will adjust accordingly. A resident's tier payment reflects their peak land ownership during the previous month and is charged by Linden Lab automatically each month. Residents can view their current land holdings, tier and account information from the My Account page of the Second Life website.

A Second Life **Private Estate** is managed and operated separately from the Mainland. Estate owners purchase from Linden Lab entire regions (private islands) away from the Mainland either for their own use or to divide then sell or rent sub-divisions to other residents.

Estate owners are able to control many more aspects of their land than can Mainland landowners. Private estate owners may for example, adjust or halt the sun cycle, change the region rating or regulate the number or avatars permitted on sim (40 max. on a Mainland region against 100 max. on a private island). Estate owners can also add a *covenant* to a region designating their own specific estate rules and conditions (see page 123).

Finding land for sale

Residents have several choices when it comes to identifying land for sale.

From Search

The **Land Sales** tab of the **Search** window ([Ctrl] + [F]) displays a list of all the land parcels that residents have up for sale.

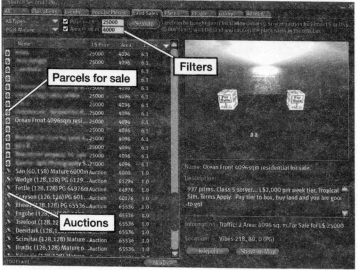

The **All Types** and **PG & Mature** drop-down menus can be used to filter these results by the type of land sale (i.e. Mainland, Estate or Auction) and by the region rating. The results can be filtered further by parcel area and price by entering a maximum spend and/or a minimum area into the relevant filter field.

From the World Map

When we tick the **Land for Sale** checkbox on the World Map legend, areas on the World Map ([Ctrl] + [M]) that are overlain in yellow identify land parcels for sale. Areas on the World Map that are overlain in purple indicate land parcels for Second Life auction (see below).

The small $ price-tag icon often seen within an overlain area can be clicked on in order to display some basic details of the sale.

Parcel for sale (yellow)

Click sale icon for basic details

Parcel for auction (purple)

It is imperative to carefully examine any land parcel you are interested in purchasing in order to ascertain that the parcel is well suited to our own purposes. Make the following checks (from within the parcel) prior to confirming any land purchase:

♦ Select **World > About Land** from the viewer's top menu bar and confirm the parcel's **Area** figure from the **General** tab. This value describes the size of the parcel in square metres.

♦ From the **Objects** tab of the About Land window examine the **Primitives Parcel Supports** figure. This is one of the most important values to consider as it indicates how many prims may be placed on this parcel (the parcel's prim limit).

♦ To ensure that we are aware of the exact size and shape of the parcel, we can display the parcel boundaries from either the viewer's top toolbar **View > Property Lines** or by using the keyboard shortcut [Ctrl] + [Alt] + [Shift] + [P].

- If large or numerous objects are obscuring your view of the parcel then we can hide pretty much everything except the land itself by displaying the viewer's **Advanced** menu ([Ctrl] + [Alt] + [D]) then un-selecting **Advanced > Rendering > Types > Volume** ([Ctrl] + [Alt] + [Shift] + [9]).

Buying land in Second Life

When we are on a parcel that is for sale we can purchase it by clicking the **Buy** icon 🔲 on the viewer's top menu bar or **Buy Land...** on the **General** tab of the parcel's **About Land** window.

The **Buy Land** window opens, displaying the full details of the transaction and also informing the purchaser whether completing the transaction will require them to upgrade their Second Life account and/or commit them to an increased monthly tier.

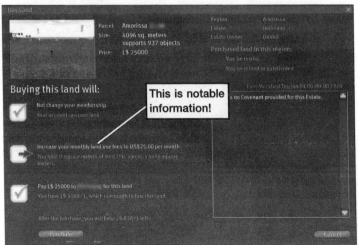

Buying a parcel on the Mainland

The transaction is completed by clicking the **Purchase** button.

Buying land from private estates

When considering buying land within a private estate it is crucial to be aware that there are fundamental differences between buying Mainland parcels and private estate parcels.

Parcels within private estates are governed by estate coven-
ants. These may outline conditions such as themes, payment terms,
rules, regulations and permitted behaviours within the estate
boundaries. Before being permitted to buy the land parcel the
purchaser may need to agree to them by ticking the **I Agree to the
Covenant Defined Above** checkbox. Always ensure that you read,
understand and accept the estate covenant before you buy any
parcel. If you do not adhere to any regulation contained within a
private estate covenant then you run the real risk of being evicted
from your parcel without discussion or refund.

Read the covenant!

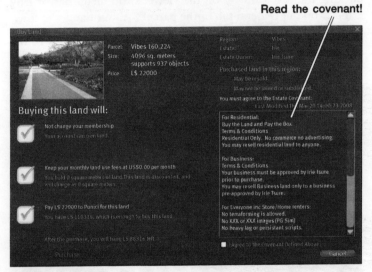

Buying a parcel on a private estate

One of the potential benefits to buying land in a private region is
that land management fees (tier charges) are charged independently from Second Life, i.e. buying land in a private region does
not affect a resident's Second Life account land tier rating. Therefore a resident need not necessarily subscribe to a Premium Second Life account in order to own a land parcel within a Private
Estate. However the Private Estate owner is almost certain to
levy their own tier charge.

One of the potential down-sides to buying land in a Private Region is that the Estate owner can evict a resident and reclaim the
parcel at any time.

Irie warning!

Do not buy land parcels within private regions if you are not totally confident in the reliability of the Estate owner. We too regularly hear the sorry tales of leaseholders being evicted with no notice even when long periods of tier have been paid in advance. Linden Lab will not involve themselves in any such dispute and the evicted resident has no open avenue of redress. Also if an estate owner does not maintain their own tier payments to Linden Lab you will lose your parcel when the region is reclaimed.

Buying land by auction

New Mainland regions and repossessed parcels are released to residents by Linden Lab through an auction system accessed via the Second Life website. Residents may enter a maximum bid for a parcel then the automatic auctioning system will bid in turn for each resident until their maximum bid is reached. At the end of the auction the successful bidder's account will be charged and the land parcel assigned to them.

Buying a private region

Residents can buy their own Second Life regions (known as Private Islands) from the **Land Store** which is accessible via the Second Life website.

Selling land in Second Life

Residents can set for sale any land parcel they own (or that their group owns if they have been granted the ability to sell group land) with a click on the **Sell Land...** button on the **General** tab of the parcel's **About Land** window. **The Sell Land** window opens into which we enter the details of the sale.

Within the **Set a price:** field we enter the price (in Linden dollars) at which we want to sell the parcel. The cost per square metre is automatically calculated and displayed alongside this field.

We specify whether we want to sell the land to anyone or to a particular Resident from the **Sell the land to:** drop-down menu.

Irie warning!

If you ever intend to sell a land parcel to a specific Second Life resident (especially if at a knock-down price) then always ensure that you select 'Specific user:' from the **Sell the land to:** drop-down menu. Some cunning residents operate perfectly legitimate software that detects bargain land parcels the moment they become publicly available.

By selecting one of the radio buttons in the **Sell the objects with the land?** section of the **Sell Land** window, the seller also has the option to transfer to the purchaser any objects that they own on the parcel (subject to each object's permissions). This is particularly useful when selling a parcel that includes a building and/or landscaping. We can highlight any objects that will change ownership by clicking the **Show Objects** button.

Click on the **Set Land For Sale** button to confirm the details and set the parcel for sale. Unless the land is set for sale to a specific resident the parcel will automatically be displayed within the listings of the **Land Sales** tab of the Search window ([Ctrl] + [F]).

Managing virtual land

Owning land allows residents to control and manage much of what happens on their parcels. We can access both useful information and many land functions from the About Land window of each land parcel we own.

Irie note

For group-owned land the parcel 'owner' refers to those group members who have been granted the ability to perform the described function.

From within a parcel you own, access the **About Land** window:

* With a click on the parcel name in the viewer's top menu bar.

* With a right-click on the parcel itself then selecting **About Land** from the pie menu.

* By selecting **World > About Land** from the viewer's top menu bar.

The General tab

The **General** tab of the **About Land** window displays basic information about the parcel and the controls to sell and deed your land.

The text inputted into the **Name:** and **Description:** fields appears in directory listings in the Search window should the owner choose to list the parcel in the directory.

The **Owner:** field displays your name on your land.

Any group associated with the land is displayed in the **Group:** field. Setting land to a group (using the **Set...** button) is most commonly applied to grant other members certain abilities, for example to build, place objects or to run scripts on the parcel.

Irie note

Setting your land to a group does **not** transfer either the ownership of or financial responsibility for the parcel.

When we set a parcel that we own to a group both the **Allow Deed to Group:** and the **Owner Makes Contribution With Deed:** checkboxes become active. *Deeding* land donates the parcel to the set group. *Contributing* with the deed donates to the group the required land use fee to maintain the deeded land. Donated tier is charged automatically to the donating resident's account.

Irie warning!

Deeding your land to a group transfers to that group both ownership and financial responsibility for the parcel. If the group does not maintain its tier commitments then the land will be reclaimed.

The **Sell Land:** button (see **Selling Land in Second Life** page 119).

The **Claimed:** field displays the date the parcel last changed ownership.

The **Area:** field displays the parcel's area in square metres.

The **Traffic:** field displays the previous day's traffic figure. A parcel's traffic figure reflects how many residents visited the parcel and for how long they stayed.

The **Buy Land:**, **Buy For Group:** and **Buy Pass:** buttons are not available for parcels that you own.

The **Abandon Land:** button relinquishes a resident's ownership to the parcel. I suggest that you never abandon land that you can no longer maintain but instead consider giving it to another resident or deeding it to a group – if you cannot find anyone to take it then give me a call (wink, wink).

The Covenant tab

The **Covenant** tab contains information about the region's covenant. Private Estate owners use this covenant in order to display any terms and conditions that residents must observe when buying or renting parcels within the Estate. Mainland parcels do not have a covenant.

The **Region:** field displays the name of the region in which the parcel is located.

The **Estate:** field displays the name of the Estate in which the parcel is located.

The **Estate Owner:** field displays the name of the owner of the Estate in which the parcel is located.

The Objects tab

The **Objects** tab displays information about objects within the parcel and within the region in which the parcel is located.

The **Simulator primitive usage:** field displays both the total number of the parcel owner's prims currently within all parcels they own within that region and the parcel owner's prim limit for that region.

The **Primitives parcel supports:** field displays the maximum number of prims that can be placed on the parcel (the parcel prim limit).

The **Primitives on parcel:** field displays the total number of prims currently within the parcel. The elements of this figure are presented in further fields:

* The **Owned by parcel owner** field displays the total number of the parcel owner's prims.

* The **Set to group:** field displays the total number of prims currently within the parcel that are set to its 'set' group.

* The **Owned by others:** field displays the total number of prims currently within the parcel that are owned by people other than the owner and/or not set to the parcel's set group (if it is set to a group).

- The **Selected/sat upon:** field displays the number of objects that are currently selected or sat upon by residents. Selected and sat upon objects (such as vehicles) do not count against the parcel's prim limit.

Entering a number (of minutes) into the **Autoreturn other residents' objects:** field will automatically return all objects on the parcel that are owned by others (see above). The minutes value in this field sets the delay between the offending object being rendered and returned.

From the **Object Owners:** section the parcel owner may click the **Refresh List** button to display a list of the residents who own prims on the parcel and the total number of prims they currently have within it. The parcel owner can then return a specific resident's objects by selecting their name from the list and clicking the **Return objects…** button.

The Options tab

The About Land window's **Options** tab is where the parcel owner dictates what abilities and permissions other residents have within the parcel.

The **Allow other residents to:** section of the Options tab offers the parcel owner the following options:

- I cannot imagine the circumstances that would possess an owner to tick the **Edit Terrain:** checkbox and permit all other Second Life residents to edit their parcel's topography.

- Ticking the **Create Landmarks:** checkbox will permit other residents to create their own landmark for the parcel.

- Ticking the **Fly:** checkbox allows other residents to start flying from within the parcel. When unchecked, other residents may still fly into and over the parcel but cannot *start* flying from within the parcel.

- By ticking the appropriate **Create Objects:** checkbox, parcel owners can specify whether all other residents and/or group members (when the parcel is either set to or owned by the same group) are permitted to create and edit objects within the parcel.

- By selecting the appropriate **Object Entry:** checkbox, parcel owners can specify whether objects owned by all other residents and/or objects owned by group members (when the parcel is either set to or owned by the same group) are permitted to cross the parcel boundary and enter the parcel.

- By selecting the appropriate **Run Scripts:** checkbox, parcel owners can specify whether all other residents and/or group members (if appropriate) are permitted to run scripted objects (such as personal dance chimeras, scripted vehicles and scripted weapons) within the parcel.

The **Land Options:** section of the Options tab offers the parcel owner the following options:

- Avatar damage is a feature most commonly used when residents are engaging in multi-player combat games in combat-defined regions. Owners can disable damage in their parcels by ticking the **Safe (no damage):** checkbox.

- Collisions are one of the physics features of the Second Life grid. To avoid disruptive or aggressive behaviour on a parcel the owner can prevent pushing (caused by collisions) by ticking the **Restrict Pushing:** checkbox.

- Parcel owners may choose to list a parcel they own in Search (places) by ticking the **Show Place in Search (L$30/week) under:** checkbox then choosing a category from the adjacent drop-down menu.

- The parcel owner is required to tick the **Mature Content:** checkbox if the parcel contains mature content (as described on page 114).

- The parcel owner may select an image to represent the parcel by clicking on the **Snapshot:** panel then selecting an image or texture to display. The picture will be displayed on the parcel's landmarks and with its listing in the search directory.

- The parcel owner decides precisely whereabouts on the parcel visiting residents will first arrive by positioning their own avatar on the desired location then clicking the **Landing Point: Set** button.

The **Teleport Routing:** drop-down menu offers the parcel owner three teleport options:

- **Blocked** prevents all other residents from teleporting to the parcel.

- **Landing Point** ensures that all residents teleporting to the parcel arrive at the parcel's specified landing point.

- **Anywhere** permits residents to teleport to any location within the parcel.

The Media tab

The **Media** tab allows parcel owners to display web pages and images within the parcel, and also to broadcast web-based movies and audio.

Irie note

Currently media displayed in-world is non-interactive, i.e. residents cannot click the links or press the buttons of web pages when they are displayed in-world.

The parcel owner sets the URL of the media to display on the parcel by clicking the **Media URL: Set...** button then entering a URL into the displayed pop-up Media URL: field. The Second Life viewer will attempt to determine the type of media we enter in this field, however the **Media Type:** drop-down menu allows the parcel owner to stipulate the media type. The parcel owner may also choose to add a brief text description of the media within the **Description:** field.

Clicking the **Replace Texture:** panel allows the parcel owner to select a texture that when rendered on the parcel will display or broadcast the parcels' set media.

The Media Options section

Ticking the **Auto scale:** checkbox automatically scales and aligns the media to fit within the surface on which the media is being displayed.

A video or sound file will automatically start again when the **Loop Media:** checkbox is selected.

Ticking the **Hide Media URL:** checkbox permits the parcel owner to conceal the media URL from other residents (except for web pages).

Ticking the **Hide Music URL:** checkbox permits the parcel owner to conceal the music URL from other residents.

The parcel owner can define the size of a displayed video, image or web page by inputting its dimensions (in pixels) within the **Media Size:** fields.

The parcel owner can broadcast music across the parcel by entering the stream address into the **Music URL:** field.

By ticking the **Restrict spatialized sound to this parcel:** checkbox, the parcel owner can ensure that sounds produced outside the parcel cannot be heard from within it and that sounds produced from within cannot be heard from outside.

The Access tab

The **Access** tab allows the parcel owner to control resident access to the parcel.

The parcel owner may allow all other residents access to the land parcel by ticking the **Allow Public Access:** checkbox. By ticking the relevant checkbox from the **Block Access By:** subsection, the parcel owner can then restrict parcel access based on whether Linden Lab has a resident's payment information on file and/or whether the resident is an age-verified adult.

When the **Allow Public Access:** checkbox is not ticked and the parcel is set or owned by a group then the **Allow Group Access:** checkbox becomes available permitting parcel access to be restricted to the set group.

When the **Allow Public Access:** checkbox is not ticked then the **Sell passes to:** checkbox becomes available allowing the owner to sell passes that permit access to the parcel for a set duration. Passes can be sold either to all residents or (if the parcel is set to or owned by a group) exclusively to group members.

When the **Allow Public Access:** checkbox is not ticked, the parcel owner may add specific residents to the **Allowed Residents** list by clicking the **Add...** button then selecting a resident by name from the displayed **Choose Resident** window.

The parcel owner may ban specific residents from the parcel by adding them to the **Banned Residents** list by clicking the **Add...** button then selecting the resident by name from the **Choose Resident** window. The parcel owner can also eject and ban residents from the parcel by right-clicking directly on the offender's avatar then selecting **More > Eject...** from their pie menu.

The parcel owner can remove residents from the **Allowed** and **Banned Resident** lists by selecting their name then clicking the **Remove** button.

The Edit Terrain menu

Editing Second Life topography is commonly referred to as *terraforming*. A parcel can normally only be terraformed by its owner. The parcel owner can also divide a parcel and if a resident owns two or more adjacent parcels then the owner is able to join the parcels together. Editing Second Life land in any of these ways is managed using the Edit Terrain tool.

Residents access their Edit Terrain menu with a right-click on the ground of their parcel then selecting **Edit Terrain** from its pie menu. If large or numerous objects are obscuring the parcel we can hide everything except the land by displaying the viewer's **Advanced** menu ([Ctrl] + [Alt] + [D]) then unselecting **Advanced > Rendering > Types > Volume** ([Ctrl] + [Alt] + [Shift] + [9]).

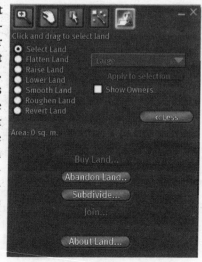

Parcel owners can flatten, raise, lower, smooth or roughen their land. These terraforming effects can be applied to land using one of the following three methods.

To terraform the entire parcel:

1 Select the desired effect radio button, e.g. **Raise Land**.

2 Click the **Apply to selection** button.

In this case, the entire parcel will be raised by approximately a metre.

To terraform a rectangular area within the parcel:

1 Select the **Select Land** radio button.

2 Click on the land, hold down the left button then drag out a rectangle.

3 Release the button when you are happy with the size of the selection.

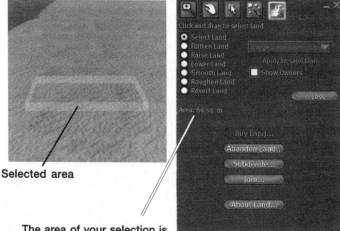

Selected area

The area of your selection is
displayed on the Edit Terrain menu

4 Select the desired effect radio button, e.g. **Raise Land**.

5 Click the **Apply to selection** button.

In this example, the land within the selection will be raised by approximately a metre.

To terraform freehand:

1 Select **Small**, **Medium** or **Large** from the terraforming drop-down menu to choose the size of the area on which you want to apply the terraforming effect.

2 Select the desired effect radio button, e.g. Raise Land.

3 Left-click on the land to apply the effect directly.

4 Hold down the left button to apply the effect continuously.

The **Revert Land** option returns a parcel's or a selection's topography to its original 'baked' (recorded) state.

Irie warning!

Be ultra-careful and confirm that you have selected the intended area of land **before** applying any terraforming effect!

Though owners can easily return the topography of a parcel to its original shape, there is no practical method of undoing a single terrain editing step. I have accidently flattened an entire region on a couple of occasions (laying waste to months of tinkering) and this type of terraforming error is both heart-breaking to encounter and time-consuming to remedy.

Ticking the **Show Owners** checkbox applies the following useful colour code to land:

• Bright green land is owned by you.

• Red land is owned by other residents.

• Blue-green land is owned by a group of which you are a member.

• Orange land is for sale.

• Purple land is for sale by auction.

Dividing a parcel

The parcel owner may wish to divide a parcel, for example to sell or rent to other residents.

To divide a parcel:

1 Select the **Select Land** radio button.

2 Click on the land, hold down the left button then drag out a rectangle.

3 Release the button when you are happy with the size of the selection.

4 Click the **Subdivide** button.

The smallest parcel residents may create is 16 sq m.

Joining parcels

When a resident wants to join together two or more adjacent parcels that they own they simply select the **Select Land** radio button, drag a rectangle to overlap the parcels they wish to join then click the **Join** button.

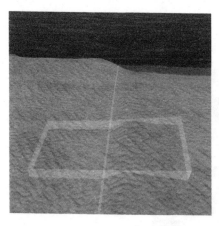

Joining two parcels

The **Abandon Land:** button relinquishes a resident's ownership to the parcel. I suggest that you never abandon land that you can no longer maintain but instead consider giving it to another resident or deeding it to a group.

08

building in second life

In this chapter you will learn:

- how to create, reshape, cut, copy and join prims
- about the importance of using the rulers and grids
- how to give an object features and properties such as flexi and light

Building in Second Life

I've cast aside a number of titles and articles discussing creating content for Second Life as it seems to be held (by commentators that have apparently never attempted to learn) that to create content in Second Life there are difficult and complex skills to master. This irritates me because it dissuades would-be builders from learning but just isn't true. Granted building takes a little time to study and practise but building is super simple once you know how! And scripting is even easier!! (See Chapter 10.)

My dream is that building, texturing and scripting objects are soon given their rightful position as basic and entry-level skills that the majority of Second Life residents quickly acquire. For Second Life is a creative heaven. With the appropriate skills a resident can construct everything. With practised texturing skills the resident can then make their creation look authentic and with the knowledge to script the object, the resident can then code the object to perform a range of imaginative tasks and functions. When (if) the time comes that a significant proportion of residents have these simple skills at their fingertips then the quality of all our Second Life experiences will be utterly transformed.

I define producing content for Second Life as creating functional art. The art created for virtual worlds is not only expected to work on a 3D visual level (and that can be tricky enough sometimes) but is greatly improved with both functionality and interactivity. For example, as a resident of Second Life I may choose to create a visually stunningly parcel; a work of art no doubt, but if other residents also find the environment easy to navigate and come across absorbing and stimulating activities that both prolong their visits to my installation and encourage their return, then my art functions well and is (in my opinion) massively improved. When an economic element is introduced into the assessment, we see that self-financing or profitable creations can be judged to be further improved when assessed as functioning works of art.

Second Life is an original and innovative medium that demands original and innovative skills, imaginings and vision. Linden Lab has created this medium; the metaphoric paint, brushes and canvas, but never forget that it is we residents who are the artists.

Functional Art? (see also Colour plate 4)

To reiterate, all objects in Second Life are constructed from individual primitive shapes referred to as *prims*. These prims are the building blocks of Second Life and can be transformed by stretching, cutting, hollowing, etc. and then joined together to fashion more complex objects and structures.

Where can we build?

Residents always possess the ability to build within the parcels that they own. If you do not own a land parcel then you are going to need to find some suitable land in order to learn to build. In order to avoid litter, most parcel owners will prohibit other residents from building on their land and so you will need to find an area where every Second Life resident can build. Such an area is known as a *sandbox*.

A sandbox is a public parcel or region provided by both Linden Lab and benevolent residents so that all residents may learn, build their objects and then test them. To locate a sandbox, we open the World Map ([Ctrl] + [M]) and enter the term 'sandbox' into the box by the Search button. When we click the Search button the list of Sandbox regions will be displayed. Residents can locate sandbox parcels by entering the term 'sandbox' under the **Places** tab of the Search window ([Ctrl] + [F]).

To avoid clutter, any object created or placed within a sandbox will be returned to its owner after a set period of time (the object will be returned to the *Lost and Found* folder of the object owner's Inventory). The time delay before an object will be returned can be established from the parcel's About Land window (see page 121).

When we use a public sandbox it is good manners to tidy up after ourselves.

What do we build?

Some months ago a resident was struggling for the necessary inspiration to help him devise some innovative objects for Second Life. 'Everything is built already!' he complained to me.

'We've only just started.' I replied. 'Nothing is built!'

Only a few years into the project, the surface of the creative pool of Second Life has barely been disturbed. I often feel that those currently creating content within Second Life are experiencing a phenomenon not unlike the discovery of fire; we know our discovery has heaps of applications, we are uncovering them fast but really and truly, we've only just started. Little has yet been created and that which has been created will be vastly improved. Our virtual world remains in its infancy.

Gleaning inspiration, ideas and solutions from real-world products or other residents' creations is all very well but we should always be as original as possible when creating content in order to respect the intellectual property rights of others. For example, creating a pair of training shoes inspired by the latest designs by Nike seems perfectly reasonable to me (for this happens on our high streets all the time). But copying their products and/or for example, putting the Nike logo or Swoosh on your Second Life product potentially leaves you open to real-world legal action whether you are selling them or not!

Irie tip

Copyright law is complex and does vary between territories. Input the search term 'copyright law' (or similar) plus the name of your country into your preferred search engine to learn more about copyright law within your local territory.

The Second Life terms of service (TOS) grant to residents the copyright and intellectual property rights over original and personally created content.

How do we build?

The viewer provides inbuilt tools for creating in-world objects.

Find a parcel on which you have the ability to build, right-click the ground to access the land's pie menu then select **Create**. The arrow cursor will transform into a magic wand and the **Creation** menu will be displayed. We can alternatively use the keyboard shortcut **[Ctrl] + [4]** to access the **Creation** menu or click the **Build** button in the bottom toolbar (if active).

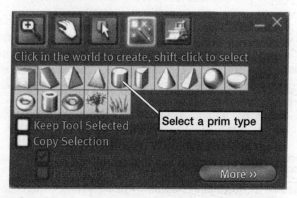

The Creation menu

Irie tip

In order to avoid being disturbed when building I routinely set my tag to **Busy**. Busy mode hides local chat, IMs, invitations, inventory deliveries pop-ups, etc. We set ourselves Busy by selecting **World > Set Busy** from the top menu bar. Residents IMing, sending inventory or invitations to a Busy resident will see a pop-up explaining that the resident they contacted is busy. We may edit our own response message in the **Busy Mode Response:** field found on the **Communications** tab of the **Preferences** window (**[Ctrl] + [P]**).

Click on the appropriate icon to select a default prim shape then with a left-click, touch the wand cursor onto either the ground or the top of an existing object and our new prim will materialize. The technical expression for this materialization is for the prim to *render* and more colloquially *rez*.

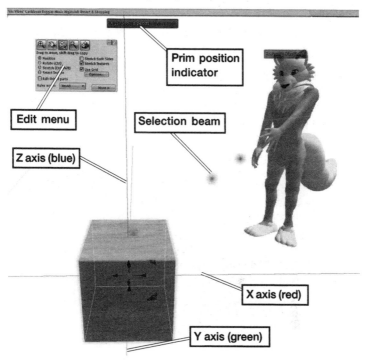

Edit menu

Prim position indicator

Selection beam

Z axis (blue)

X axis (red)

Y axis (green)

Our example avatar's first creation (see also Colour plate 5)

We see the newly created prim and also our example avatar's selection beam.

Irie tip

Our example avatar has changed the colour of his selection beam. This is managed from the **General** tab of the **Preferences** window (**[Ctrl] + [P]**) by clicking on the **Color For My Effects** panel then using the colour picker.

The newly created prim is outlined in yellow and surrounded by lines, arrows and triangles. This indicates that it is selected. You should also notice that the **Creation** menu has become the **Edit** menu and the **Tools** option appears in the viewer's top menu bar.

Its position on the region is displayed as X, Y and Z coordinates at the top centre of the viewer. A sim measures 256m × 256m and the coordinates are expressed in metres from 0.000–256.000 for the X (red) and Y (green) axes. The Z (blue) axis indicates its altitude, between 0 and 768 metres.

The Edit and some other menus can be expanded by clicking the **More >>** button and reduced by clicking the **<<Less** button.

Within the expanded section are found the menu's tabs.

When a new prim is rendered it is named 'Object' by default and set to the creator's active group (or none if no group is active).

The following basic primitive types can be produced using the **Creation** menu.

The cube

Just like its real world counterpart, the brick, the cube (or box) is our most fundamental and oft-used building block. For convenience some variations (edited cubes) are also available directly from the Creation menu. These are the **prism, pyramid** and **tetrahedron**.

Cube, prism, pyramid and tetrahedron

The cylinder

The cylinder is essentially a rounded cube. For convenience some cylinder variations are also available directly from the Creation menu. These are the **hemicylinder**, **cone** and **hemicone**.

Hemicone, cone, hemicylinder and cylinder

The cube and cylinder are considered members of one prim family (i.e. the cube family) and therefore share the same editing options. A second group of prims, the Sphere family, offer a different set of editing tools which in some cases are not available to apply to members of the cube family.

The sphere

Spheres (and family) allow builders to incorporate curves into objects and are therefore helpful for instilling interest and flow into a creation and are also useful for creating objects with a more organic appearance. For convenience, a **hemisphere** is available directly from the Creation menu.

Sphere and hemisphere

The torus

The torus is my favourite default prim shape. Somewhat doughnut or bead shaped, tori (plural) prove to be versatile in offering a host of shaping possibilities in the hands of the practised builder. I use tori to create a wide variety of shapes ranging between delicate hair curls and ten-metre carved columns.

The tube and ring

Both the tube and ring are similar in appearance to a hollowed-out cylinder but as they are members of the sphere family, they offer different editing and shaping options to cube family cylinders.

Tube and ring

Irie tip

Take the time to examine these prim shapes and their variations. The more familiar you are with Second Life's basic building blocks then the more proficient you will be as a content creator.

Landscaping from the Creation menu

Residents can also create trees, plants and patches of grass directly from the Creation menu. When either the tree or the grass icon is selected a seemingly random item of flora is rendered when the creation wand is clicked on the ground of the parcel.

All flora are available as individually named items from within the Library section of the Inventory. Linden Landscaping can be incredibly useful for residents as each tree, plant or patch of grass only counts as a single prim against the parcel's prim limit.

Irie tip

A large area can be landscaped in just a few moments by ticking the **Keep Tool Selected** checkbox on the Creation Menu then clicking the wand repeatedly on the ground.

An introduction to sculpted prims

Sculpted prims are used to create more complex, organic shaped prims that are not possible with the default prim system. A sculpted prim's shape is described by the RGB (Red, Green, Blue) values in an image file (a Sculpt Texture or Sculpt Map) which as a result appears as a strangely beautiful rainbow texture.

Currently, I create sculpted prims externally using the free 3D modelling software Blender (www.blender.org) and Wings 3D (www.wings3d.com). I then convert the model into a Second Life sculpt map (using an exporter plug-in) and upload this into Second Life (as an image file). The imported sculpt map is applied to a prim from its **Object** tab by selecting **Sculpted** from the **Building Block Type** drop-down menu then selecting the new sculpt texture using the **Sculpt Texture** panel.

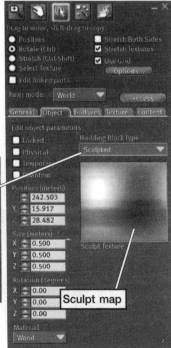

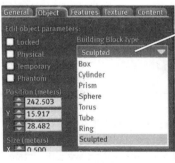

Wings 3D is easy to learn and well suited for making sculpted prims. You will find the sculpt map exporter plug-in for Wings 3D by entering the search-term 'sculpty exporter for Wings 3D' or similar into your preferred search engine. This enables us to produce a Second Life sculpt map directly from the 3D modelling software.

If you get more involved with creating sculpted prims there is little doubt that you will want to put the time and effort into learning the more complex Blender software (or similar). Free and with all the features of the expensive programs, Blender is my preferred software. However, be warned, Blender does take some time and effort to master though both the manual and tutorials are available online from the Blender website.

To get a sense of what is possible with sculpted prims take a look in the *library* folder of your inventory and you will find some excellent examples of sculpted prim creations. This wonderfully detailed sculpted fruit bowl by Qarl Linden is in there (see also Colour plate 6).

Irie prediction

I have little doubt that in the not too distant future, solutions for creating sculpted prims in-world will become freely available.

Deleting and taking prims

Residents should take care to clear up after themselves. We can take any object (a prim or group of linked prims) that we have created into our inventory by selecting the object (see below) then selecting **Take** from the object's pie menu. On the other hand if we do not wish to keep the object then we can delete it straight into our inventory's Trash folder.

There are two ways to delete an object:

* By selecting the prim then pressing [Delete].
* By right-clicking the object then selecting **More > Delete** from its pie menu.

Irie note

If you try to delete an object and after a few moments it remains visible then it has 'ghosted'. It's not really there and if you log out of the grid, it will be gone when you return. You can ignore it or may be able to move it out of the way.

Selecting objects

Other than by creating a prim there are two other methods to select an object or number of objects.

* **With a Click:** Right-clicking an object then selecting **Edit** from its pie menu will select a single object. **[Shift]** + left-clicking other objects will progressively select them into a group (the selected prims are outlined in bright yellow).
* **With a Box:** When in edit mode (**[Ctrl] + [3]**), holding down the left button then dragging the cursor causes a yellow rectangle to form which selects the objects within its boundaries. We can repeat this action to select additional objects. This is not only the best method to quickly select many objects but is also wonderful for locating and selecting those that we or other residents have lost underground.

When we mistakenly select an object into a group, then **[Shift]** + click on the offending object deselects it from the group.

Irie tip

If someone else's object gets selected along with your own it is unlikely that any further group modifications will be possible (e.g. we will almost certainly not be able to move the group). It is therefore often practical to select **Tools > Select Only My Objects** from the viewer's top menu bar before running a group selection.

Linking prims

Residents can link up to 256 prims together in order to construct more complex objects. We link a number of prims by selecting them as a group, then by selecting **Tools** > **Link** from the top menu bar or with the keyboard shortcut [Ctrl] + [L]. A linked object cannot normally exceed 30 metres in any aspect.

The order in which we link prims is significant as all the prims in an object are assigned a link number (this can be important when scripting). The final prim selected to the group becomes the *root* or *parent* prim and remains outlined in bright yellow. The other or *child* prims of the linked object are outlined in light blue.

We unlink the prims of our selected linked object either by selecting **Tools** > **Unlink** from the top menu bar or with the keyboard shortcut [Ctrl] + [Shift] + [L].

Positioning an object

Three axis lines (red, green and blue) intersect at the geometric centre of a selected object. Each axis contains two cone-shaped arrowheads (handles) of the same colour. The positive direction of an axis (i.e. towards 256.000 on the X or Y axes and up on the Z axis) is indicated by the direction of the arrow on these position handles.

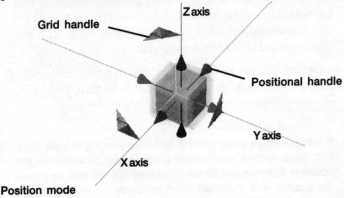

Position mode

The X axis is a red line, the Y axis is a green line and the Z axis is a blue line.

Each position handle is selectable and will both brighten in colour and increase in size when the cursor is positioned over it. Holding down the left button then dragging a positional handle will cause the object to move along the selected axis.

We can also reposition an object from the **Edit** menu by opening the **Object** tab and altering the values in the **Position (meters)** X, Y and Z input fields.

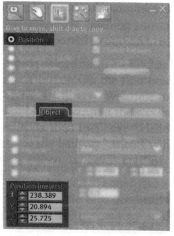

Changing these position values on the Object tab moves the object in-world

Rotating an object

Selecting an object then holding down [Ctrl] allows us to rotate the object. When in rotation mode, colour coded X,Y and Z axis rings are displayed around a semi-transparent globe that appears either around or inside your selected object depending on your camera view. We may also select the Edit menu's **Rotate** radio button to enter rotation mode.

Rotation ring

Each colour-coded rotation ring is selectable and will both brighten in colour and increase in size when the mouse cursor is positioned over it. Left-clicking and dragging a rotation ring causes the other rotation rings and the globe to disappear and the object to rotate accordingly around the selected axis.

Free rotation is managed by clicking on then dragging across the semi-transparent globe and in my experience only happens by accident as (for me) this method rotates the object uncontrollably on several axes at once.

We can also rotate an object (much like when positioning one) from the **Edit** menu by altering the values in the **Rotation (degrees)** X, Y and Z input fields under the **Edit** menu's **Object** tab.

Irie note

Members of the cube family are initially rendered at 0° on all three axes but members of the sphere family are initially rendered at 90° on the Y axis. My guess is that this is so tori, tubes and rings are initially rendered with an 'upright' appearance but there may be some more mathematical explanation that I'm unaware of.

Stretching and scaling

How we may resize an object depends on whether it is a single prim object or one comprised of a linked group of prims. Linked groups can only be scaled proportionally larger or smaller but cannot be stretched along a single axis.

Irie note

A single prim may not be stretched to any dimension either below 0.010 metres or above 10.000 metres.

Stretching a prim

Selecting a prim then holding down [Ctrl] + [Shift] allows us to resize it. In Stretch mode, little colour-coded cubes are displayed around the prim and at the top of the viewer are displayed the X, Y and Z dimensions of the selected object. We may also select the Edit menu's **Stretch** radio button to enter stretch mode.

Resizing handles

The sizing handles are colour-coded to indicate on which axis the object will be resized. The grey cubes at the corners of the selected object allow us to scale the prim or object proportionately. When we select and drag a sizing handle the object will stretch or scale along the respective axis.

Irie note

When the selected object is comprised of a linked group of prims then only the grey sizing handles are displayed because multi-prim objects cannot be stretched along a single axis.

Ticking the **Stretch Both Sides** radio button on the selected object's **Edit** menu causes any resizing to be applied equally along the selected axis. When un-ticked the selected prim will only be resized in the direction the sizing handle is dragged.

We can also resize a prim using the **Size** input fields on the object tab of the selected object's **Edit** menu. When using these input fields the selected prim will always be resized equally on both sides.

Undo and Redo

Undo ([Ctrl] + [Z]) has my vote as being the single most useful function we builders have at our disposal. Each object within Second Life records the actions performed upon it and this allows us to quickly remedy editing mistakes and also encourages us to explore modifications as we can simply and immediately undo those we don't like.

Irie note

We must close any active chat or IM fields in order that the Undo and Redo commands apply to our building and not to our chat!

This wonderful function also allows us to move an object (perhaps blocking our access to something underneath) and then once we are finished tinkering elsewhere (regardless of the amount of other building and editing we do during the intervening period) to reselect the interfering object, 'undo the move' and replace the object quickly and perfectly back in its original location.

Repeatedly pressing [Ctrl] + [Z] or [Ctrl] + [Y] (Redo) undoes or redoes the selected object's most recent moves and edits one at a time and in the order they occurred.

The rulers and building grid

High quality creativity within Second Life relies as much on our precision as it does on our imagination. You can be as artistic as Picasso but if you can't position your prims precisely then your work will still look a mess. Builders manage the accurate positioning and sizing of prims by using the rulers and grids provided within the viewer.

Ruler mode

From an object's **Edit** menu we can select **World, Local** or **Reference** from the **Ruler Mode** drop-down menu.

- **World** is the default ruler mode and when selected, irrespective of the object's orientation, the ruler and grid are displayed relative to the Second Life region. For example, when the object is in World ruler mode, dragging it along the red X axis will always move it east or west, in turn dragging the object along the green Y axis will always move it north or south and dragging it along the blue Z axis will always move the object vertically up or down. In the same way, when an object is in World ruler mode, rotating the object using the colour-coded rings will rotate the object around axes relative to the region.

- When **Local** ruler mode is selected, the ruler and grid are displayed relative to the current orientation of the selected object. For example, when in Local ruler mode, dragging an object along the X axis will move it forward or backwards relative to its current orientation, in turn dragging an object along the Y axis will move it from side to side relative to its orientation and dragging it along the Z axis will still move it up and or down but now relative to its own orientation. When an object is in Local ruler mode, using the colour-coded rings rotates the object around its own local X, Y and Z axes.

- The **Reference** ruler mode does appear to be very useful but I'm not sure I've used it to provide a practical solution (yet). When the Reference ruler mode is selected, typing **[Shift]** + **[G]** fixes a reference grid based on the object's current coordinates and orientation. Whilst in this mode, further rulers and grids will be orientated to these reference coordinates and axes irrespective to the orientation of the next selected object.

Irie tip

It is best to reposition your view to drag objects from side to side or up and down. Dragging a prim towards or away from the camera position runs the risk of losing control of the movement and the object disappearing off into the distance.

The building grid

There is no better way to maintain perfection and develop building speed than with proficient use of the grid. In this instance we are not discussing the Second Life grid but instead the Second Life viewer's building grid. This allows builders to resize prims quickly to specific measurements and position objects rapidly to precise coordinates and orientations.

To use the building grid we must tick the **Use Grid** checkbox on the **Edit** menu ([Ctrl] + [3]). The building grid increments, and how far the grid extends, can both be adjusted by clicking the **Options…** button beneath the **Use Grid** checkbox.

By axis

When we are using the building grid, as soon as we start to drag an object along an axis by selecting one of the colour-coded handles, a ruler appears either side of the selected axis.

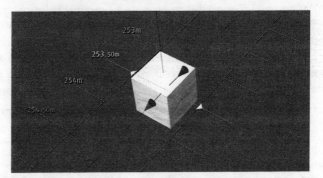

Move your cursor into either ruler to snap the prim into precise positions

An object will move freely along an axis when we drag it by its positional handle. Free movement occurs when the cursor remains in between the two rulers. However if we drag the cursor into either ruler, then drag the object, it will incrementally and precisely snap along the axis between the ruler's marks. As the cursor drops back between the rulers then free movement is restored.

By plane

When an object is selected and depending on your view, up to three twin-colour triangles, the object's 'grid handles', appear in between the axis lines.

Grid handle

An object's grid handles permit us to move the object in increments simultaneously along two planes. As soon as we select a grid handle, the building grid will appear on the relevant plane and when we move the selected object it will snap precisely to this grid.

Irie tip

When commencing a build, I will always snap the initial prim to the grid on all three axes by using the grid handles. This makes the perfect positioning of additional prims a snapping task rather than the more complex and time-consuming process of inputting coordinates.

By rotation

Builders also use a ruler to precisely rotate their objects. As soon as we start to rotate an object around an axis by selecting one of the colour-coded axis rings, a ruler appears around the axis ring indicating the degrees of rotation around the selected object. When we move the cursor into this ruler, our object will rotate in increments making it easier to be precise.

By scale

Builders also use a ruler to precisely stretch or scale their objects. As soon as we start to scale an object by selecting one of the colour-coded scaling cubes, a ruler appears either side of the selected axis. When we move the cursor into this ruler, our object will stretch or scale in increments making it easier to be precise.

Editing linked parts

There are often moments in building when we need to edit a single prim within an object composed of a linked group of prims. Of course we could unlink the group, edit the prim then re-link the group but this is not necessary. We edit an individual prim in a linked group by ticking the **Edit Linked Parts** checkbox found on the selected object's Edit menu.

When this checkbox is ticked, with a click we can select any individual prim in the group then edit it in any way we could with an unlinked prim with the following provisos:

- We cannot move a linked prim beyond the link limit distance (usually 30 metres).

- We cannot delete a linked prim.

- We cannot copy a linked prim.

- We cannot unlink the root prim (highlighted in bright yellow).

By holding down [Shift], we can select additional prims to edit from the linked group, for example in order to collectively move, scale or unlink the prims.

Copying objects

Copying an object is obviously much quicker than building a new one. We can copy any object that either we have created ourselves or that we own and has the *Copy* item permission enabled (see page 74). There are several ways to copy an object.

Using the [Shift] key

In almost all building situations the most practical method of copying an object is to select the object, hold down [Shift] then drag the object away from its original position using one of the object's position or grid handles. This moves the selected object but leaves an exact copy of it in its original location.

Irie tip

The Local Ruler Mode works well in conjunction with the [Shift] key method of copying, as the axes will relate to the orientation of the original object and the ruler will reflect the exact dimensions of the original object. This permits us to perfectly and quickly position and align copies of an object however irregular its original size and orientation.

By duplication

We can also create a copy of a selected object by selecting **Edit** > **Duplicate** from the viewer's top menu bar (keyboard shortcut [**Ctrl**] + [**D**]). The duplicate object will be rendered offset from the original object by half a metre on both the X and Y axes.

By selection

We can create a copy of a selected object from the Creation menu ([**Ctrl**] + [**4**]) using the following method.

1 Select the object to copy.

2 Open the **Creation** menu by clicking the 'wand' icon at the top of the **Edit** menu or with the shortcut [**Ctrl**] + [**4**].

3 Tick the **Copy Selection** checkbox.

4 Touch the wand cursor on any suitable surface and a copy of the selected object will be rendered where clicked.

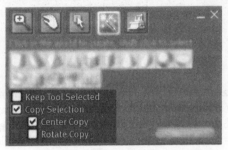

When the **Centre Copy** checkbox is also ticked, the copy will render aligned to and touching any prim on which we click.

We can quickly create a number of copies by ticking the **Keep Tool Selected** checkbox. When this is ticked a copy will be rendered each time we click on any suitable surface.

From Inventory

The least practical method of copying an object (when building) is to take the object into inventory (right-click > **Take**) then rendering copies in-world (by dragging them from inventory and onto a suitable surface) as they are required.

Object parameters

On the Object tab of the expanded Edit menu ([Ctrl] + [3]) is a section labelled **Edit object parameters:**.

Within it are four checkboxes:

* When an object has the **Locked** checkbox ticked the object unsurprisingly becomes locked and even the owner is not able to move, resize or texture it. If we try to delete a locked object

a dialog box appears to ask for confirmation. I most commonly lock buildings and other large objects in order to avoid accidents as I continue to build in and around them.

* When an object has the **Physical** checkbox ticked it will become susceptible to the Second Life physics engine. For example gravity will affect it, collisions will cause it to react and hollowed objects will appear to weigh less than solid ones.

* When an object has the **Temporary** checkbox ticked it will persist in-world for up to three minutes and then be deleted from the Second Life grid. This parameter is most commonly used for objects such as bullets or footprints that once created are designed to quickly disappear. I also use this to tidy up a number of unruly prims such as after a multi-ball football match (i.e. select football, tick **Temporary**, left-click next football, tick **Temporary**, left-click next football and so on).

* When an object has the **Phantom** checkbox ticked then avatars and other objects are able to pass right through it.

Material types

On the **Object** tab of the expanded **Edit** menu there is a **Materials** drop-down menu. By default, when we create a prim, it will act as though it is made of wood, e.g. it will sound chunkier than glass when it is bumped into.

We may change a prim's material from wood to stone, metal, glass, flesh, plastic or rubber. The behaviour of the different materials can be subtle and is most easily observed when the object is rendered physical (i.e. has the **Physical** checkbox ticked).

Prim editing

Prims can be edited to offer Second Life's builders an almost infinite variety of shapes with which to construct. We edit a selected prim from the **Object** tab of its **Edit** menu ([Ctrl] + [3]).

The various editing functions displayed on the **Edit** menu depend on which prim type is selected.

Prim type

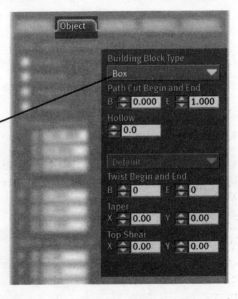

Editing a box

Path cut

Path cutting may be applied to any prim type and acts to reduce the selected prim around its vertical axis.

We define the degree of reduction using the Path Cut B (begin) and E (end) input fields.

Either or both of these input fields may be used to reduce the prim as each applies the cut in an opposite direction.

Hollow

Hollowing may be applied to any prim type and acts to create a space emanating from the geometric centre of the prim.

We define the degree of hollowing in increments from 0.0 (solid) to 95.00(%).

When hollowed, most prim types become hollow inside, but hollowing a cube or a cylinder creates an opening straight through it.

When we hollow out a prim the default hole shape will be a close relative of the prim shape (e.g. a square hollow for a cube or a circular hollow for a sphere). However we can also choose to redefine the shape of the hollow using the **Hollow Shape** drop-down menu.

In this example I used the Hollow Shape drop-down menu to create a circular 60% hollow within a cube prim.

Twist

Twist may be applied around the Z axis of any prim type.

I applied 'shininess' (see texturing) to these prims to improve your view of the twist

We dictate the degree of twist using the B (begin) and E (end) input fields.

Cube family prims can be twisted through 360° (0 to +/-180), while the sphere, torus, tube and ring can be twisted through 720° (0 to +/-360).

Taper

Taper may be applied to any prim type *except the sphere* (i.e. the Taper edit fields do not appear on a sphere's edit menu). It is used to narrow the prim on the X and Y axes.

We define the degree of taper using either or both the X (axis) or Y (axis) input fields.

The torus, tube and ring appear to taper very differently from members of the cube family as they appear to split then narrow around the circumference of the prim.

Top shear

Top shear may be applied to any prim type *except the sphere* and is used to offset the top surface of the prim relative to the bottom surface.

We define the degree of this offset using either or both the X (axis) or Y (axis) input fields.

Dimple

Dimples can *only* be applied to a sphere prim and acts to reduce the sphere along the X axis by opening a cone-shaped cavity to the sphere's core.

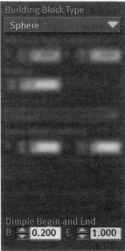

We define the amount of dimple applied using the B (begin) and E (end) input fields. Either or both of these input fields may be used to reduce the prim as each applies a dimple from opposite sides of the sphere and in an opposite direction.

Hole size

Hole size can *only* be applied to a torus, tube and ring and is used to edit the dimensions of the prim's existing hole.

We define the hole size using either or both the X (axis) or Y (axis) input fields.

Profile cut

Profile cut can *only* be applied to a torus, tube and ring and is used to reduce the prim around its X and Y axis.

We define the amount of profile cut in the B (begin) and E (end) input fields.

Either or both of these input fields may be used to reduce the prim as each applies their cut from opposite ends of the prim and in an opposite direction.

Skew

Skew (next to Hollow) can *only* be applied to a torus, tube and ring and acts to slice the prim then draw the two ends apart along the X axis.

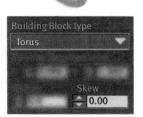

We define the skew in increments from –0.95 to 0.0 (no skew) to +0.95.

Radius

Radius can *only* be applied to a torus, tube and ring and acts to slice the prim then draw the two ends apart along the Y axis.

The amount of radius we can apply to a prim is dependent on Hole Size Y and may only be applied where it is less than 0.50.

Revolutions

Revolutions can *only* be applied to a torus, tube and ring and are used to create up to four turns around a prim's X axis.

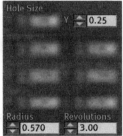

The next step

We have now examined all the default prim shapes and the individual editing functions that can be applied to them. The next step, and one that you must undertake by yourself, is to start to explore the effects of applying these edits in combination. For example the Radius, Revolutions and Hole Size settings seem to produce the most effective and useful shapes when they are applied in combination with each other.

By applying various editing functions in combination we learn how to create an infinite array of prim shapes and some quite startling and surprising effects.

Prim features

The *features* of flexibility and light can be applied to prims in order to enhance their functionality, effect and authenticity.

Irie note

Prim features must be applied to individual prims, therefore when working on a linked group, the **Edit linked parts** checkbox must be ticked and then a single prim selected prior to applying the desired feature.

Adding flexible properties to a prim

Assigning flexible or *flexi* properties to prims adds an enormous degree of dynamism and realism to objects such as flags, prim clothing, flora, etc. With flexi applied, these objects appear floppy and react to both Second Life gravity and wind.

Irie note

Flexi prims are always Phantom in nature and additionally cannot have their Physics parameter enabled.

We assign the various flexible properties to a prim by initially ticking the **Flexible Path** checkbox found on the **Features** tab of the selected prim's **Edit** menu then adjusting the various values within the input fields beneath.

Exploration and discovery will prove your best strategy to grasp the effects of applying varying degrees of the following flexible path properties. Flexi properties are easiest to observe on stretched prims such as the elongated cube used in the previous image.

• **Softness** is applied in whole number values ranging from 0 to 3. A softness value of 0 results in a very solid and erect prim whilst entering a softness value of 3 results in a prim that behaves more like wet lettuce.

• **Gravity** is applied in values ranging from –10.0 to +10.0. The gravity value dictates the degree of downward force (or upward force for negative values) exerted on the prim with the value of 0.0 being weightless or zero gravity.

• **Drag** is applied in values ranging from 0.0 to +10.0. The drag value dictates how air friction affects the movement. A drag value of 0.0 results in a very 'whippy' and responsive prim whilst a drag value of 10.0 results in the prim responding in a more relaxed and flowing manner.

• **Wind** is applied in values ranging from 0.0 to +10.0. The wind value dictates how the prim is affected by the wind's strength and direction. A value of 0.0 results in no reaction to wind whilst a value of 10.0 results in the prim responding wildly to the wind as though it were made of tissue paper.

• **Tension** is applied in values ranging from 0.0 to 10.0. The tension value dictates how much stiffness is applied to the prim. A tension value of 0.0 results in a very floppy prim whilst a tension value of 10.0 results in a very stiff prim.

• **Force X, Y, Z** is applied in values ranging from –10.0 to +10.0. The force value dictates the degree of directional force exerted on the prim with the value of 0.0 being neutral. The force value allows us to apply a directional force to a flexi prim and is perfect when we want to allow our prim to flutter in the breeze, but only in a certain direction, for example to keep hanging curtains away from seating.

Irie tip

To see how a flexi prim reacts we need to move it. To save time while you explore the various flexible properties, rather than repeatedly dragging the prim around, move it just the once and then move it as you require using the [Ctrl] + [Z] and [Ctrl] + [Y] shortcuts.

Adding light properties to a prim

Assigning light properties allows us to create objects that both radiate light and illuminate the surrounding environment.

Residents control the detail of the lighting displayed by the viewer from the **Graphics** tab of the **Preferences** window ([Ctrl] + [P]). Ticking the **Custom** checkbox on the **Graphics** tab displays various options including a section titled **Lighting Detail:**. Residents require the **Nearby local lights** radio button to be selected to see prim lighting.

We cause a prim to emit light by ticking the **Light** checkbox found on the **Features** tab of the selected prim's **Edit** menu, selecting a colour from the **Color** palette then adjusting the various values within the input fields beneath.

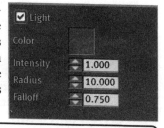

Irie tip

The effects of a prim's light properties are easiest to observe in the dark. Select **World > Force Sun > Midnight** from the Second Life viewer top menu bar.

As always, experimentation will prove the best method to grasp the effects of applying varying degrees of the light properties.

• **Color** [*sic*] is applied to the light with a click on the panel then selecting a colour from the displayed colour picker. Changing the colour of the emitted light often changes the colour of the object.

- ◆ **Intensity** dictates how much light is emitted from the prim and is applied to the light in values ranging between 0.000 (no light) and 1.000 (max. light).

- ◆ **Radius** dictates the reach of the emitted light and is set by inputting a value between 0.000 and 20.000 metres. The path of the light emitted from a prim is not interrupted by objects such as walls and floors therefore we use Radius to restrict a light's spread.

- ◆ **Falloff** applies a diminishing intensity gradient along the light's path in values between 0.000 and 2.000. A value of 0.000 applies no falloff and the light will display at full intensity within the entire radius. A value of 2.000 applies maximum falloff and the light intensity quickly diminishes towards the radius.

Building summary

Building is the art of combining our prim editing and our prim manipulation skills to create beautiful, imaginative and/or functional objects.

To evolve as an innovative builder it is essential to become familiar with every basic prim type and the widest possible range of shape variations and derivations each prim shape can offer. Spend time playing with prims, experimenting by combining differing degrees of cut, twist, hollow, etc. and then applying the available properties and features. This experience of the available building blocks is the most fundamental asset for any proficient Second Life builder.

Remember that there is really no practical difference between creating, positioning, shaping and a couple of prims and creating complex objects. Only practice, patience and time.

Irie's building tips

- **Be diligent.** In order to broaden your building 'vocabulary', take the time to explore prim variations and features, learn new skills and then practise them.

- **Build as you require.** Save money and learn at the same time. If you need a new sofa then build a new sofa!

- **Be innovative.** Improve objects that are available and develop products that are not.

- **Use the building grid.** Build precisely by wherever possible using the rulers and building grid provided.

- **Build using regularly sized prims.** When practical, build using prims of regular dimensions (1.0m, 1.25m, 5.0m, etc.) and placed at regular angles (0°, 45°, 90°, etc.) to make the positioning, aligning and texturing of prims a simple process.

- **Become a perfectionist.** Do not tolerate unintentional gaps, overlaps or other errors in your building.

- **Build in good light.** Fix the sun to an appropriate position to build your object then view it under different lighting conditions (e.g. **World > Environment Settings > Midday**).

- **Build a module library.** When you create a building element that either you particularly like or feel could be useful again then link it into a single object, name it well then take a copy of the object into your inventory.

- **Set the perms.** Never transfer an object to another resident without carefully checking that you are comfortable with the state of the item permissions.

- **Check functionality.** Create an Alt (alternative account) to check the object works as intended with other avatars.

- **Remain at the cutting edge.** Take the time to keep abreast of Second Life's new tools and features via the Second Life blog. Visit other creators' stores and view their content to glean their latest thinking and solutions.

- **Become part of the Second Life creative community.** Second Life permits, no encourages, us to surround ourselves with creative individuals. Chat with and engage those content creators you admire and also those residents (like us) who aspire to create high quality objects.

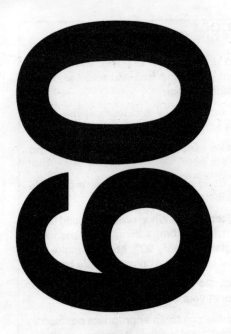

09

texturing

In this chapter you will learn:

- how to texture a prim or object
- about the features offered on the Texture tab
- about the different faces on an object

Texturing an object

I've heard and said myself that a great build is 90% in the texturing. I have no idea how accurate the statement is but it certainly makes the right point and therefore I have little hesitation in suggesting that when it comes to creating content for Second Life, high quality texturing is the most important skill to develop.

Textures are not only applied to add an appropriate surface appearance to an object but also to enhance realism and dimension, to reduce prim usage and make an ordinary object look fantastic. Almost any **jpg**, **gif**, **bmp**, **png** or **tga** image can be used to texture an object.

The Texture tab

I am sure you have noticed that a newly created prim is textured with Second Life's default plywood texture and uncoloured. We edit the texture and colour of a selected object from the **Texture** tab of its **Edit** menu ([Ctrl] + [3]).

The **Texture** panel displays the thumbnail of the texture currently applied to the selected object. Click this to display the **Pick: Texture** window.

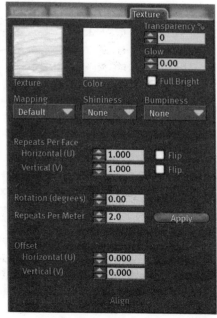

Within the **Pick: Texture** window is a larger texture panel, again displaying the currently selected texture and also the image's dimensions (in pixels).

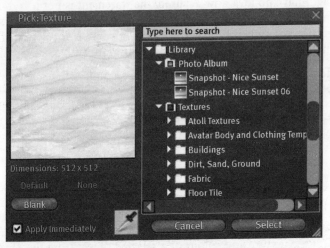

* Clicking the **Default** button replaces the texture within the panel with the default texture.

* Clicking the **Blank** button replaces the texture within the panel with a plain white texture.

* The **None** button only becomes available when texturing 'Skins' and when clicked removes the texture image from a skin (if you don't know what I'm talking about then this button is not important).

Irie note

Be careful! There are NO [Ctrl] + [Z] (Undo) and [Ctrl] + [Y] (Redo) functions available when texturing.

Only *Inventory* and *Library* folders containing textures are displayed in the **Pick: Texture** window's **Texture Inventory**. Textures are searched for here in the same way as from the regular inventory, then the choice confirmed by clicking the **Select** button. The selected texture will then be displayed in the large panel of the **Pick: Texture** window.

The **Apply Immediately** checkbox is ticked by default and when ticked any selected texture is instantly applied to the selected surface. When this checkbox is not ticked, we will need to click the **Select** button to apply the selected texture.

The panel labelled **Color** [*sic*] displays the colour (default white) currently applied to the selected object and with a click on the panel we can access a standard colour picker.

The **Apply Immediately** checkbox is ticked by default and when ticked any selected colour is instantly applied to the selected surface. When this checkbox is not ticked, we will need to click the **Select** button to apply the selected colour. The selected colour will be applied evenly to the selected surface and is likely to affect the appearance of any applied texture.

Irie tip

Both the Colour Picker and the Pick: Texture window offer an Eyedropper function. Click the icon and the texture or colour displayed on the surface we next click on will be copied to the selected surface (subject to permissions).

Transparency is applied to a surface from the Transparency input field using whole values ranging from 0 to 90 (%). A value of 0 is fully opaque whilst the maximum value of 90 results in a texture appearing almost completely transparent.

When we want an object to appear completely transparent we can use one of the 100% transparent textures provided in **Inventory > Library > Textures**.

Irie tip

If you misplace a transparent object select View > Highlight Transparent or use the keyboard shortcut [Ctrl] + [Alt] + [T]. Once selected all the transparent surfaces in view will get a bright red overlay making them easy to locate.

Glow is applied to a texture from the **Glow** input field using values ranging from 0.00 (no glow) to 1.00 (maximum glow).

Increasing the value creates an aura around the prim. I find that the Glow feature is perfect for producing effective light and flame effects especially when applied at very low (fluorescent) values such as 0.02.

Ticking the **Full Bright** checkbox causes the selected texture to appear illuminated during darkness. Full Bright is a particularly useful feature to apply to signs and lighting effects that we wish to be eye-catching under all light conditions.

Irie note

Ticking the Full Bright checkbox does not cause the selected object to emit light.

Effectively combining the Glow and Full Bright features with Textures, Colours and Light (see also Colour plate 7)

Surface options

Below the Texture and Color panels we see three drop-down menus.

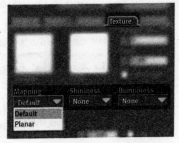

The Mapping menu

Editing the shape of a prim can cause the texture to appear scaled, seamed and/or distorted. For example to correct the distorted texture from a tapered cube prim, we select Planar from the Mapping drop-down menu and our texture is then applied uniformly to the plane of the surface rather than compressed within the proportions of prim faces.

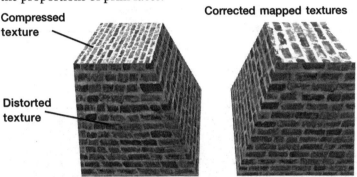

Compressed
texture

Corrected mapped textures

Distorted
texture

The Shininess menu

Shininess places a reflection of the Second Life skyline on your object. The effect is largely dependent on the available light and your viewing angle. One of four levels of shininess can be applied to a texture: None, Low, Medium, or High.

None

The higher the Shininess setting selected then the darker the object will appear and the brighter the reflection becomes.

Irie note

Residents control how they view features of an object's detail from the Graphics tab of their Preferences window ([Ctrl] + [P]). Objects will only appear shiny to residents who have ticked the Bump Mapping and Shiny checkbox in the Shaders: section (tick the Custom checkbox to view).

The Bumpiness menu

This applies a bump map texture to the surface of an object and is used to produce a more authentic grained appearance.

None

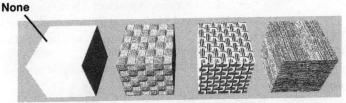

Selecting any option other than **None** from the **Bumpiness** drop-down menu applies the respective bump map to the object and very effectively produces a surface with a more tactile appearance. The **Brightness** and **Darkness** options enhance the bumpiness of the existing texture and therefore do nothing when no texture is applied to the surface.

The settings in the remainder of the Texture tab are used to control the size and placement of the texture image *and* any selected bump map, therefore any adjustments we make in this section are applied equally to both the texture *and* any selected bump map.

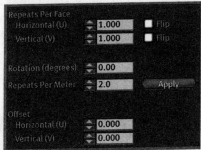

Repeats Per Face

The Repeats Per Face section of the Edit menu is used to adjust the scale of any applied texture and/or bump map on either or both the Horizontal (U) and Vertical (V) axes. The figures within these input fields reflect and are used to adjust the number of times that the texture will be repeated across a surface, therefore the larger the number inputted then the smaller the texture will appear. We may assign a value from 0.00 to 100.00 repetitions across either axis.

A texture can also be reversed across a surface horizontally or vertically by ticking the relevant **Flip** checkbox.

Rotation (degrees)

The Rotation input field reflects the texture's current rotation and is used to adjust the rotation of any applied texture and/or bump map. Textures can be rotated in one degree increments from −180 to +180.

Repeats per Meter

The Repeats per Meter function applies scale to a texture without reference to the dimensions of the surface to which it is applied. This is useful when matching textures across objects of different sizes. We can enter values between 0.1 and 10.0 repeats per metre into the input field. We then click the adjacent **Apply** button to assign this scale to the texture and/or bump map.

Offset

The Offset fields allow us to adjust the placement of the texture by shifting it along either or both the Horizontal (U) and Vertical (V) axes. Textures can be shifted by entering values from −1.000 to 0.000 (no shift) to +1.000.

Regarding faces

A *face* is defined as any prim surface to which a texture can be individually applied. A prim (depending on its shape) can have up to nine different faces. Each face can have a different texture applied to it and then edited individually using any of the features and functions contained on the object's texture tab.

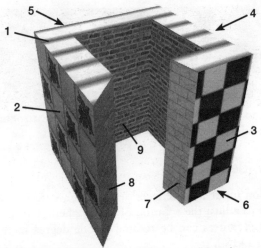

Any surfaces inside a hollowed prim are considered as a single face

To apply or edit a texture to an individual face we first select the **Select Texture** radio button on the **Edit** menu.

To then select an individual face we simply left-click on it. Once selected, each texture repetition on the selected face and its placement are outlined in white with each texture's centre marked with a white and crossed circle. These guide marks illustrate the scale, offset and rotation of each texture on the selected face of the object. We may now use all the functions offered within the Edit Menu's texture tab to individually edit the selected face.

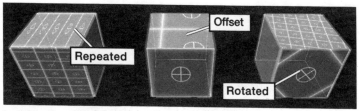

Individually edited faces

Additional faces may be selected to edit several faces as a group. We select addition faces to a group by holding down [Shift] then clicking the face or faces we wish to add to the edit. Holding down [Shift] then clicking on a selected face will de-select it.

Stretch textures

Within a selected object's Edit menu is the **Stretch Textures** checkbox. When the object is resized this checkbox determines the effect of the resizing on its texture.

When ticked and the selected object is resized, then the texture **Repetitions per face** value will remain unchanged and the texture will resize to reflect the object's revised dimensions.

When the **Stretch Textures** checkbox is not ticked and the selected object is scaled or stretched then the texture **Repeats per meter** value will remain unchanged and the texture will not resize.

Z flutter

Z flutter occurs when two or more prims render a face on an identical plane and the Second Life viewer attempts to display them together resulting in an unattractive flickering effect. We eliminate Z flutter by fractionally repositioning one of the prims so the offending faces occupy separate planes.

Texturing sculpted prims

A sculpted prim has just one texture face. Any texture can be applied to this face using the prim's Texture tab. Experiment between default and planar mapping as planar mapping can appear better as with this sculpted hair-wrap.

Sculpted prims tend to be irregularly shaped and unlike my simple hair-wrap (above) a single sculpted prim may need to represent more than one type of material. For example, part of a sculpted prim may be metal; while another part may be wood. This makes texturing sculpted prims a complicated process.

Texturing summary

Our eye has an uncanny ability to accept the shapes and patterns it expects and to highlight the unusual. This means that within the visually immersive environment that is Second Life, simplistic, mismatched, poorly scaled, irregular or just plain lazy texturing will be noticed. It also means that when we spend the time to competently texture an object then the result can be enormously effective and pleasing.

Irie's texturing tips

- Don't spend time on texturing an object until you have completed or nearly completed it.

- Then take the time to apply textures perfectly.

- Texture in the most suitable light.

- Experiment with bump mapping, shininess, mapping, etc. to determine what features improve our objects.

- Do not overuse the Glow and Full Bright features as you will dilute their effectiveness.

- Position your avatar alongside the textured object to get a sense of scale and perspective.

- Examine each face then edit it individually as required.

- Collect free and very cheap textures in-world.

- Produce your own textures!

- We produce our own textures to use within Second Life using software such as the GIMP (my personal favourite because it's both free and packed with functionality).

10

understanding scripting

In this chapter you will learn:

- how to compile and run a script
- how a script operates
- how to write an efficient script

Scripts

Scripts allow Second Life objects to move, listen, talk, operate as a vehicle or weapon, change colour, size or shape and to perform a whole host of other functions.

Linden Scripting Language (LSL) is the code used to script the objects we encounter and make in Second Life. A script can be placed inside any in-world object but not inside an avatar. However avatars can and routinely do wear scripted objects such as HUDs, radars, chimeras, bling jewellery, etc.

Compiling and running a script

Scripts can only run from within an object so in order to compile and run a script we must first create a new prim.

1 Create a new prim.

2 Select the **Content** tab from the new prim's **Edit** menu.

3 Click the **New Script** button to create a default script within the object.

4 Close the **Edit** menu.

You will notice the text 'Object: Hello, Avatar!' has been broadcast in open chat. Left-click the object and 'Object: Touched.' is broadcast in chat. Taaaa daaaa! You have just compiled and run an LSL script.

An introduction to scripting

If you already understand how computer programming works then this section can largely be ignored. If scripting is completely new to you then it becomes vital that you understand this simple section before proceeding further.

Grasping the basic principles of scripting proved to be the thorniest branch of my Second Life learning experience. I spent the weekend between Christmas and New Year with my head in the LSL Wiki, digesting article after article and tutorial after tutorial on the subject and for much of the weekend I just didn't get it. Eventually the light came on and my progression towards becoming a proficient scripter at once became rapid. But it is an incredibly simple principle to grasp with the right analogy.

So I want to create a useful picture in your imagination...

Imagine a house. It is a very grand house indeed. It is your home (lucky you!). At the front of this house is a large entrance hallway. This entrance hallway is your 'home' or default location and every time you appear, you arrive in this hallway.

In this entrance hallway are two boxes. Written on the first box are the words 'When you arrive, I will say "Hello, Avatar"'. Written on the second box are the words 'If you touch me, then I will say "Touched."'. And basically that is how a script works.

Open the default script, i.e. the one you created in your first scripted object or use **Create > New Script** from the Inventory top menu bar then right-click > Open the 'New Script' created in the inventory *Scripts* folder. Adjust the window as necessary to make the entire script visible and you should see the following:

This default script is our imaginary 'hallway' expressed in LSL

```
Script: New Script                               _ X
  File   Edit   Help

default
{
    state_entry()
    {
        llSay(0, "Hello, Avatar!");
    }

    touch_start(integer total_number)
    {
        llSay(0, "Touched.");
    }
}



Line 0, Column 0
                                          Save

☑ Running                              Reset
```

In LSL, our imaginary hallway is referred to as a *state* (as is every imaginary room). In this script our hallway is the default state and anything that occurs in our hallway (or default state) is contained between the container (the matched { and }) closest to the left margin. A script must contain a default state as when a script is either started or reset it must start in its default state.

```
Default
{
   ......
}
```

Our two imaginary boxes in the entrance hall are referred to as the script *events*. In the default script these two boxes (or events) are expressed in LSL as:

```
state_entry()
{
   ......
}
```

A **state_entry** event is the first event triggered when the state (imaginary room) is entered.

and...

```
touch_start(integer num_detected)
{
   ......
}
```

A **touch_start** event is triggered when the object is touched.

Anything that might happen when either event is triggered is contained in the subsequent container (matched { and }).

In the default script, a *function* will be called when either event is triggered. These functions are expressed in LSL as:

```
llSay(0, "Hello, Avatar!");
```

This particular function commands the object to say 'Hello, Avatar!' in general chat.

And...

```
llSay(0, "Touched.");
```

This function commands the object to say 'Touched.' in general chat.

Are you with me so far? If so let me create a second useful image in your imagination...

Remember our grand entrance hallway with the two boxes? I hope so. We are now going to change what is written on one of the boxes in our hallway. The first box still reads 'When you arrive, I will say "Hello, Avatar!"'. But now written on the second box are the words 'If you touch me, firstly I will say "Sending you to the kitchen" then I will transport you directly to the kitchen.'

Let us imagine we touch this 'new' second box. The box obediently says 'Sending you to the kitchen' and we are then magically transported to our kitchen.

Arriving in the kitchen we hear the words 'Welcome to the kitchen Avatar!' and discover two new boxes. On the first box are written the words 'When you arrive, I will say "Welcome to the kitchen Avatar!"' (Ah! This explains the state entry message we just heard). On the second box are written the words 'If you touch me I will firstly say "Sending you to the hallway" then I will transport you directly back to the hallway.'

Let us imagine we touch this second box. The box obediently says "Sending you to the hallway" and then we are magically transported back to the hallway. When we arrive in the hallway, of course, the first box in the hallway notices our entry and says "Hello, Avatar!".

The following is our current imagining expressed in LSL.

```
Default
{
  state_entry()
  {
    llSay(0, "Hello, Avatar!");
  }

  touch_start(integer num_detected)
  {
    llSay(0, "Sending you to the kitchen");
    state kitchen;
  }
}
```

```
state kitchen
{
  state_entry()
  {
    llSay(0, "Welcome to the kitchen Avatar!");
  }
  touch_start(integer num_detected)
  {
    llSay(0, "Sending you to the hallway");
    state default;
  }
}
```

The significant difference between this script and the default script is that within this second script there are two states; the default state (imaginary hallway) and the kitchen state.

Let us first examine the contents of the default state (contained within the first container (closest to the left margin).

The first event is the **state_entry** event and is identical to the **state_entry** event in the default script.

The second event is a **touch_start** event and contains the following two functions:

```
llSay(0, "Sending you to the kitchen");
```

This commands our object to say 'Sending you to the kitchen'.

```
state kitchen;
```

This function calls our script to change state to 'kitchen'.

Irie note

Logic dictates that in our imaginary home we can only exist in one room at any one time and as such a script can only be in one state at any one time. Our script can be in either the default state or the kitchen state. The script can move between states but the script cannot be in both states.

Examine the 'kitchen' state now. Pretty simple isn't it? If not then start reading this chapter again.

Exactly copy this *kitchen* script into a new script and click the **Save** button. You should see the message 'Compile successful, saving...' appear in the box below the script editing area. After a short pause you should see the message 'Save complete' appear there. If you received any error messages when saving or running a script, check and double-check for accuracy. It is most likely that you have omitted or added a curly bracket or missed a semicolon at the end of a function call. Brackets, parentheses, and semicolons must all be perfectly in place before a script will run.

Find the script in your inventory (it's probably still called 'New Script', right-click it and select **Rename**. Rename it something appropriate like 'kitchen script' then drag the script into the contents tab of a new prim or alternatively onto the object itself whilst holding down [Ctrl].

"Hello, Avatar!". Now touch the box. And again. And again!

The script of course is not a big imaginary house but instead is contained within this object. What is actually happening is:

1 The new script enters default state and
   a. Calls the function in **state_entry**
   b. The object says 'Hello, Avatar!'

2 The object waits to be touched.

3 When touched the script calls the functions in the **touch_start** event:
   a. The object says 'Sending you to the kitchen'
   b. The script enters kitchen state.

4 The script calls the function in the 'state_entry' event:
   a. The object says 'Welcome to the kitchen Avatar!'

5 The object waits to be touched.

6 When touched the script calls the functions in the **touch_start** event:
   a. The object says 'Sending you to the hallway'.
   b. The script enters default state.

7 ...and the whole process starts again.

Important things to know about scripting

Nesting

A nested container is one included within another. Indenting nested containers is not required for a script to run correctly but is commonly accepted as good practice as indenting the contents of each nested container by a further tab does make a script a lot easier to comprehend.

```
{
    {
        . . . . .
    }
}
```

Comments

A comment is most often used to help scripters explain a line of code or section of script or to temporarily obscure a line of code from the compiler (the software which changes our script into code the computer can understand). Comments are defined on a single line by using '//'. Every word to the right of '//' is considered a comment and will be ignored by the script compiler.

```
//this is a comment
//and will be ignored by the script compiler

Default //this is the state
{
    state_entry() //this is an event
    {
        llSay(0, "Hello, Avatar!"); //this is a
function
        //llSay(0, "Goodbye, Avatar!"); (this line is
commented out)
```

LSL states

A state is a section of the script that, when active, is waiting for at least one event.

• Only one state can be active at any one time.

- All scripts must have a default state with at least one event in it (many scripts *only* contain a default state).

- With the exception of the default, states can be freely named. A state is defined by the word **state** followed by its name.

- The contents of a state are enclosed between two matched curly brackets (its container).

LSL events

Events are contained within states and are either triggered by actions happening to or around the object the script resides in or alternatively triggered from within the script itself. Events run one at a time and in the order they are triggered. Once triggered the event calls the functions held within its container one at a time and in the order they are written.

We've already come across the state_entry event (triggered by the state being entered) and the touch_start event (triggered when an avatar touches an object). Unlike a state, an event cannot be freely named.

All LSL events with their trigger definitions can be found listed within the Second Life LSL Portal: **http://wiki.secondlife.com/wiki/LSL_Portal**

LSL functions

When an event is triggered then the functions held within that event's containers will be called one at a time and in their scripted order. Functions can either be user-defined or built-in. Those built into LSL all start with two lowercase Ls. We have already used the built-in function **llSay()** which commanded our object to speak. All LSL functions with their definitions and examples uses can be found listed within the Second Life LSL Portal: **http://wiki.secondlife.com/wiki/LSL_Portal**

Functions take information from the brackets () that follow them. When we position the cursor over a function in the script window, a pop-up will be displayed that tells us of what information the function is expecting and a brief description of the function performed.

```
llSay(0, "Touched.");

llSay(integer channel, string msg)
says msg on channel
```

The **llSay** function displays a pop-up that informs us that it expects two values of a specific data type; an *integer* (i.e. a whole number) to identify the channel on which the message will be broadcast and a *string* (i.e. the string of words and/or characters to broadcast). The llSay function will not accept other values.

In the example above we see the integer value is '0' (the channel for general chat) and the string value is 'Hello, Avatar!'. The result is that when this Function is called then 'Hello, Avatar!' will be broadcast on the general chat channel zero, i.e. 'says msg on channel'.

LSL data types

Integer: In LSL a valid integer value is any whole number between −2147483648 and +2147483647. Example integer values:

```
1, 5, 57, 609846
```

Float: In LSL a valid float value is any number (with or without decimals) between 1.175494351E-38 and +3.402823466E+38. Example float values:

```
1.2, 3.0, 5.97, 9.34593
```

String: In LSL a string value contains a sequence of characters. Any character may be used in a string. In LSL string values are enclosed in double quotes. Example string values:

```
"Irie Tsure"
"1234565abcdef!"£$%^"
"Hello Avatar!"
```

Key: A key is another name for the unique identifier (UUID) of every item, object and resident in Second Life. In LSL key values are enclosed in quotes. Example key value:

```
"c541c47f-e0c0-058b-ad1a-d6ae3a4584d9"
```

Vector: In LSL, a vector value is used to define a position, a speed and direction or a colour.

+ Position: x, y and z expressed in metres.

+ Velocity: x, y and z expressed in m/s.

+ Colour: x = red, y = green, z = blue.

A valid vector value contains three float values separated by commas and enclosed by < and >. Example vector value:

```
<1.00, 2.00, 3.00>
```

Rotation: In LSL a rotation value is used to define an object's orientation. A valid value contains four float values separated by commas and enclosed by < and >. Example rotation value:

```
<1.00, 2.00, 3.00, 1.00 >
```

List: A list contains a series of other valid data values separated by commas and enclosed by [and]. Example list values:

```
[0, 1, 2, 3, 4, 5]
["Caleb", "Charlton", "Elis", "Alf"]
[6, 3.141592654, "Random", < 1.0, 2.0, 3.0 >]
```

LSL constants

Constants are values that never change and are used to simplify code. Example constants:

```
PI
```
always produces a float value of:

3.1415926535897932384626433832795

```
PUBLIC_CHANNEL
```
is always channel 0

```
NULL_KEY
```
always indicates an empty key value

```
ZERO_ROTATION
```
always produces a rotation value of <0.0, 0.0, 0.0, 1.0>

All LSL constants along with their definitions can be found listed in the Second Life LSL Portal: **http://wiki.secondlife.com/wiki/LSL_Portal**

LSL flow statements

Within a script flow statements such as **if, else, do,** etc. control which code is run and when code is run. Let me create a picture in your imagination. It is so much easier.

I hope you remember our hallway and our boxes. Imagine that the first box now has written on it: 'If the owner of this box touches this box then I will say "Hello Boss!" otherwise I will say "Hello Avatar!"'. This would be expressed in LSL using flow statements as follows:

```
default
{
 touch_start(integer num_detected)
 {
  if (llDetectedKey(0) == llGetOwner())
  llSay(0, "Hello Boss!");
  else
  llSay(0, "Hello Avatar!");
 }
}
```

And broken down it works like this:

1.
```
touch_start(integer num_detected)
```

When I am touched...

2.
```
if (llDetectedKey(0) == llGetOwner())
   llSay(0, "Hello Boss!");
```
Detect the avatar and detect the object owner (two separate LSL Functions) and **if** they are identical then say 'Hello Boss!' on chat channel zero.

3.
```
else
   llSay(0, "Hello Avatar!");
```
Otherwise say 'Hello Avatar!' on chat channel zero.

All LSL flow statements, with their definitions and examples of usage, can be found listed within the Second Life LSL Portal: **http://wiki.secondlife.com/wiki/LSL_Portal**

Declaring variables

A variable is a snippet of code in a script where we store a value (i.e. a string, integer, float, vector, rotation, key, or list) in order that this information can be accessed more than once and from elsewhere in the script.

For example, within a script we can command that the text 'gOwner' should be considered a *key* by declaring the variable globally: A *global variable* is declared before the default state (therefore will apply to all states), is customarily prefaced with a 'g' and is accessible from anywhere in the script.

```
key gOwner;

default
```

A *local variable* is declared and accessible only within the scope of a container (i.e. between a matched { and } including any further nested containers).

```
key gOwner;
default
{
 gOwner = llGetOwner();
 touch_start(integer num_detected)
 {
  if (llDetectedKey(0) == gOwner)
  {
   llSay(0, "Hello Boss!");
  }
 }
}
```

We use variables to simplify and speed up the process of running a script. Let me create yet another picture in your imagination...

In our entrance hallway are two boxes. Written on the first box are the words 'When anyone arrives, I will say "Hello Avatar"'. Written on the second box are the words "*If* the owner of this box touches this box *then* I will say "Hello Boss!" then I will say "Sending you to the kitchen" then I will transport you directly to the kitchen *otherwise* (i.e. any other avatar) I will say "Hello Avatar!".'

Let us imagine we (as the owner) touch this 'new' second box. The box obediently says 'Hello Boss!' then says 'Sending you to the kitchen' and then we are magically transported to our kitchen.

Arriving in the kitchen we hear the words 'Welcome to the kitchen Avatar!' spoken and discover two new boxes. On the first box are written the words 'When you arrive, I will say "Welcome to the kitchen Avatar!"'. On the second box are written the words 'If the owner of this box touches this box then I will say "Hello Boss!" then I will say "Sending you to the hallway" then I will transport you directly to the hallway *otherwise* I will say "Are you lost?"'.

Let us imagine we touch this second box. The box obediently says 'Hello Boss!' then says 'Sending you to the hallway' and then we are magically transported back to the hallway. When we arrive in the hallway, of course, the first box in the hallway notices our entry and says 'Hello Boss!'.

When we put these two states together into a working script, we should look to simplify the script using variables and might end up with something like the one shown on page 194.

Irie note

I hope you noticed that in our example kitchen script it is impossible for any avatar but the owner to change the script state to 'kitchen' and therefore much of the flow control within the kitchen state is redundant and is included only for the purpose of example.

The built-in LSL script editor (compiler) very kindly changes the colour of any text that it recognizes, using these colour codes.

- Maroon   States and functions
- Light blue   Events
- Blue   Flow controls (if, for, while, etc.)
- Dark blue   Constants
- Semi-light green   Type declarations (integer, string, etc.)
- Dark/pale green   Strings
- Orange   Comments

```
Script: Kitchen Script                                    _ X
 File    Edit    Help

key gOwner;
default                          Declared global variable
{
    state_entry()
    {
        llSay(0, "Hello, Avatar!");
    }

    touch_start(integer num_detected)
    {
    gOwner = llGetOwner();          Declared local variable
        if (llDetectedKey(0) == gOwner)
        {
            llSay(0, "Hello Boss!");           Variable
            llSay(0, "Sending you to the kitchen");
            state kitchen;
        }
        else
            llSay(0, "Hello Avatar!");
    }
}

state kitchen
{
    state_entry()
    {
        llSay(0, "Welcome to the kitchen Avatar!");
    }

    touch_start(integer num_detected)
    {
        gOwner = llGetOwner();
        if (llDetectedKey(0) == gOwner)
        {
            llSay(0, "Hello Boss!");
            llSay(0, "Sending you to the hallway.");
            state default;
        }
        else
        {
            llSay(0, "Are you lost?");
            state default;
        }
    }
}

Line 0, Column 0
```

See also Colour plate 8

I hope this chapter has offered a simple introduction and a clear overview of how LSL operates but please don't be fooled; most of your scripting learning is yet to come. The LSL Portal (Wiki) partners all scripters on most scripting projects as the continuous source of the information we need to make our scripts work. But you should now have the framework of understanding into which to set these elements.

The LSL Portal or Wiki (**wiki.secondlife.com/wiki/LSL_Portal**) is a ready resource for scripting solutions as well as discussing, featuring and previewing the latest developments and thinking around LSL.

Debugging

There are plenty of errors that can prevent a script from running properly or from running at all. Problems within a script are referred to as *bugs* or *glitches* and it is attention to the details that is usually the cure. The most common signal that a script is not compiling properly is when we try to save the script an error message is displayed within the Script window:

```
Script: New Script                                    _ X
  File    Edit    Help

default
{
    state_entry()
    {
        llSay(0, "Hello, Avatar!")
    |

    touch_start(integer total_number)
    {
        llSay(0, "Touched.");
    }
}

(5, 4) : ERROR : Syntax error

Line 5, Column 4

                                                       Save
☑ Running                                              Reset
```

The compiler's message displays the error type and its location within the script (line 5, character 4). In this example, I have carelessly omitted the required semi-colon that should be positioned at the end of the llSay function within the state entry event and this omission prevented the script from compiling.

How to write a script the Irie way

1 **Make the script work.** The most important aspect of a script is that it functions properly and does what we want it to do.

2 **Make the code neat and readable.** Once the script works ensure that the code is properly indented and appropriately commented.

3 **Optimize the code.** Examine the script with a view to simplification, for example by declaring variables.

Irie note

There are several example scripts in the Library section of your inventory.

appendices

A: Earning money

The Second Life economy

Since the beginning of 2007, Second Life residents have spent in-world over US$20 million every month. Tens of thousands of Second Life residents can and do create personal income streams, some worth thousands of US dollars a month.

Getting a job

As I mentioned earlier, experienced Second Life business owners are often a little reluctant to employ inexperienced and new residents. Exceptions are made within the 'adult-orientated' sectors where the only skill required is developing a presentable avatar.

In contrast, two or three months' experience combined with some appearance, social, building and scripting skills secured under the belt make any resident infinitely more attractive as an employee across a wide range of sectors.

Income from most in-world employment is token in value when compared with any real-life equivalent. The motivation of the Second Life employee is usually not to amass fortunes but to generate enough income in-world to ensure that their residency is financially self-sustaining. Employees will usually be satisfied to generate enough Linden dollars to cover their shopping bills and rent.

The other key motivation for employees is to meaningfully participate in and support a Second Life business without making a financial commitment. Many in-world businesses (including mine) rely upon such residents who are happy to support the enterprise with their regular efforts and in return to receive mostly gratitude, but in addition a few Linden dollars so that their Second Life experience never becomes a financial burden.

Some example jobs

- Store staff or management
- Nightclub host or manager
- Journalist
- DJ/Entertainer
- Security guard
- Model
- Dancer/Escort (adult industry)

Starting a business

The entrepreneurial economy of Second Life is driven by the two facts that Second Life's Terms and Conditions grant to residents the intellectual property (IP) rights of their own creations, and that Linden dollars are easily and legally exchangeable for US dollars.

Content creators are therefore able to sell their goods to other residents and service providers can be hired to provide an ever-increasing range of professional and personal services. Thousands of residents are now creating significant real-life incomes from their Second Life enterprises and the result is a vibrant marketplace of Second Life products and services.

There are bans and/or restrictions in both in-world gambling and in-world banking activities, so carefully check the Second Life TOS before venturing into either of these sectors.

By way of example, here are a few in-world businesses through which residents create part or all of their real-life income:

- Manufacturer/retailer
- Fashion designer
- Nightclub/resort owner
- Shopping mall operator
- Land/real estate
- Custom avatar designer
- Architect/landscaper
- Scripter
- Animation creator
- Publisher
- Publicist
- Event and wedding planner

Irie note

As Second Life evolves it is inevitable that more in-world employment and business opportunities will be discovered and developed. Those residents with experience and practical skills will be best positioned to benefit from this growth.

B: Troubleshooting

Here you may find solutions to some of Second Life's commonest problems:

My avatar is wearing what appears to be a newspaper.

If you hear another resident suggesting that you 're-bake' then you probably look like this:

It is unfortunate that when this happens, it will only be you that is unaware of the missing textures. The way to replace this 'Missing Image' texture with the correct texture is selecting **Character > Rebake Textures** from the Advanced Menu ([Ctrl] + [Alt] + [D]). Alternatively and when the Advanced menu is displayed, the shortcut [Ctrl] + [Alt] + [R] can be used to rebake textures.

My avatar is completely black.

If you are displaying Second Life on a secondary monitor then moving the viewer back to the primary monitor should cure this problem. You may also need to rebake your avatar's textures and perhaps restart Second Life. If not then you probably have a graphics card issue (see Chapter 2).

Who are the Cloud Avatars?

If your system has not received enough information from the region server to display another avatar properly then you will see a little cloud in their place. This 'Casper' effect usually lasts no longer than a few minutes.

How do I stop dancing (or any other persistent animation)?

There are a few ways to stop a persistent animation. Depending on how you got started, one of the following solutions should sort you out. Try them in this order.

1 If you started by (usually left-) clicking a dance machine object (or similar), then clicking the same object again will usually stop the animation.

2 Select **World > Stop All Animations** from the top menu bar.

3 If you are in a venue ask another resident for some help. Regulars may be familiar with any idiosyncrasies of the dance machine object.

4 Fly or teleport away.

5 Restart Second Life.

I cannot hear a parcel's music stream.

It can be very irritating being at a great venue when either the music stream breaks up or is not playing at all. Initially check with other residents whether they are experiencing the same problem. If they also have sound problems then the issue is probably not with you. If they are hearing the music clearly then one of the following solutions may sort you out. Try them in this order.

1 Ensure that the **Play Streaming Music When Available** checkbox is ticked on the **Audio & Video** tab of the **Preferences** window.

2 Click the play button on the music player.

3 Check your audio card and speakers are set up and work correctly.

4 Close any other applications that connect to the Internet.

5   Switch off any other networked devices that connect to the Internet.

6   Reboot both your computer system *and* the router/modem.

7   From the **Network** tab of the **Preferences** window reduce the **Maximum Bandwidth** setting to 100. If this solves the problem then incrementally increase the setting to the maximum usable value.

I seem to have lost items from my inventory.

In most instances your items are not lost but will reappear after clicking the **Clear Cache** button on the **Network** tab of the **Preferences** window. The Second Life viewer will then need to be restarted. The inventory may take a few minutes to reload but hopefully with your missing item included.

I have a hat that I want to wear but when I do it replaces my prim hair.

The hair and the hat cannot both be 'attached to skull' at the same time. From the inventory, right-click on the prim hat, select **Attach To >** then select an alternative attachment point, for example **Chin** or **Nose**. The hat will attach but be incorrectly orientated. Right-click the hat object (still attached), select **Edit** from the pie menu then rotate and position the hat into the correct orientation.

I can't find an item that I bought.

My experience as a retailer is that this is not usually an issue with the vendor but with the purchaser. One of these solutions may recover the missing item. Apply them in this order.

1   Search the inventory again using the **Recent Items** tab and/or the filtering system.

2   Check the inventory *Trash* folder. When your avatar is in Busy mode then items are delivered to *Trash*.

3   Check you haven't accidently muted either the retailer or the vending object as muting prevents the delivery of items.

4   Many retailers are sympathetic when items are lost by accident or as the result of circumstance. If your recovery efforts fail then contact the relevant retailer and politely request a

replacement. If you are unsure who to contact then look at your Second Life account's transaction history: http://www.secondlife.com/account/transactions.php

I have made an agreement with another resident but they aren't keeping to the agreed deal.

This problem covers any dispute from not receiving an item you have paid for, an estate owner reclaiming land that has been paid for, to disputes over a business arrangement. Linden Lab does not involve themselves with any such issues so be careful who you give your money to.

I am being harassed or abused by another resident.

Mute them! This is by far the simplest and most effective way of cutting off an annoying resident and I love the function so much that I am lobbying for it to be made available in the real world.

But there are visitors to Second Life whose behaviour goes beyond the merely mutable and if their conduct violates the Second Life Terms of Service or Community Standards then you can and should file an Abuse Report by selecting **Help > Report Abuse...** from the viewer's top menu bar .

C: Useful keyboard shortcuts

User Interface

[F1]	Help
[Home]	Fly
[M]	Mouselook
[Esc]	Reset to default view
[Ctrl] + [F]	Search window
[Ctrl] + [G]	Active Gestures
[Ctrl] + [H]	Chat history window
[Ctrl] + [I]	Inventory
[Ctrl] + [M]	World Map
[Ctrl] + [Shift] + [M]	Mini-Map
[Ctrl] + [P]	Preferences window
[Ctrl] + [R]	Always run
[Ctrl] + [U]	Upload image
[Ctrl] + [T]	Communicate window
[Ctrl] + [Shift] + [S]	Snapshot
[Ctrl] + [Shift] + [']	Snapshot to disk
[Ctrl] + [Shift] + [A]	Start/Stop video to disk
[Ctrl] + [Shift] + [W]	Close all windows
[Ctrl] + [Alt] + [1]	Show/hide User Interface (i.e. windows, menus etc.)
[Ctrl] + [Shift] + [1]	Show/hide Statistics window
[Ctrl] + [Alt] + [Shift] + [P]	Show/hide land parcel boundaries

Menus

[Ctrl] + [1]	Focus menu
[Ctrl] + [2]	Move menu
[Ctrl] + [3]	Edit menu

| [Ctrl] + [4] | Create menu |
| [Ctrl] + [5] | Land menu |

Editing

[G]	Snap selected object to the building grid
[H]	Focus viewer to selected object
[Ctrl] + [L]	Link selected objects
[Ctrl] + [Shift] + [L]	Unlink selected objects
[Ctrl] + [Z]	Undo
[Ctrl] + [Y]	Redo

Advanced menu

[Ctrl] + [Alt] + [D]	Show/hide Advanced menu
[Ctrl] + [Alt] + [T]	Toggle Highlight Transparent
[Ctrl] + [Alt] + [R]	Rebake textures

index